T0254578

Simulating Crowds in Egress Scenarios

Vinícius J. Cassol · Soraia R. Musse
Cláudio R. Jung · Norman I. Badler

Simulating Crowds in Egress Scenarios

 Springer

Vinícius J. Cassol
Virtual Humans Simulation Lab
Pontifical Catholic University of Rio Grande
  do Sul
Porto Alegre, Rio Grande do Sul
Brazil

Soraia R. Musse
Computer Science Department
Pontifical Catholic University of Rio Grande
  do Sul
Porto Alegre, Rio Grande do Sul
Brazil

Cláudio R. Jung
The Institute of Informatics
Federal University of Rio Grande do Sul
Porto Alegre, Rio Grande do Sul
Brazil

Norman I. Badler
Department of Computer and Information
  Science
University of Pennsylvania
Philadelphia, PA
USA

ISBN 978-3-319-87973-4   ISBN 978-3-319-65202-3   (eBook)
https://doi.org/10.1007/978-3-319-65202-3

Printed on acid-free paper

This Springer imprint is published by Springer Nature
The registered company is Springer International Publishing AG
The registered company address is: Gewerbestrasse 11, 6330 Cham, Switzerland

Contents

Chapter 1
Introduction

Enthusiasts from different areas have observed human behavior for many years, decades, or even centuries. Such observations can produce valuable data to be studied in different fields, from engineering to psychology.

In the nineteenth century, LeBon (1895) observed that, when part of a group, an individual can abandon her[1] own mental identity and assumes the identity of the group. Also, the individual can have his/her judgment affected as a function of collective behaviors around him/her. According to the author, the individuals in a crowd can discard their own values and even their inhibitions and present behaviors that should not be performed if they were alone. Such unusual behavior can engender different emotions in people. These feelings, for example, anxiety, jitters, or panic, make the individual more emotive and, sometimes, irrational. Similarly, Sighele (1954) highlights situations in which people lost reason when in crowds and act against different targets, including their own state. Both the authors discuss the power of a crowd, which can present an uncontrollable and unpredictable force.

Such emergent, often unpredictable, collective behaviors can occur when people are part of a crowd, and they can share ideas, feelings, and the same or similar goals. While the accepted definition of a crowd is a large group of people that are gathered or considered together, recent scientific studies have considered crowds as an entity able to self-organize (McPhail 1991). Examples of such collective behaviors are the spontaneous formation of lanes of uniform walking direction in bidirectional flows (Milgram et al. 1969), or the oscillation of the passing direction at narrow bottlenecks (Helbing and Molnár 1995). In addition, LeBon (1895) claims that there are several characteristics of crowd psychology: "impulsiveness, irritability, incapacity to reason, the absence of judgment of the critical spirit, the exaggeration of sentiments, and others." Le Bon claimed "that an individual immersed for some length of time in a crowd soon finds himself—either in consequence of magnetic influence

---

[1] In this book the feminine forms /her/, /hers/, and /she/ will substitute for more awkward combinations such as /him/her/, /his/hers/, /he/she/, and /she/he/.

© Springer International Publishing AG 2017
V.J. Cassol et al., *Simulating Crowds in Egress Scenarios*,
https://doi.org/10.1007/978-3-319-65202-3_1

given out by the crowd or from some other cause of which we are ignorant (in a special state), which much resembles the state of fascination in which the hypnotized individual finds himself in the hands of the hypnotizer."

The definition proposed by Sighele (1954) considers a crowd as **a heterogeneous** and *inorganic* **aggregation of people**. *Heterogeneous* usually means that a crowd consists of individuals from all ages, gender, and different social and cultural realities. A crowd is considered *inorganic* because of its capability to emerge suddenly without formal control and organization. However, the aggregated structure is important to recognize in a crowd. As observed by Thalmann and Musse (2013), aggregated motion is both beautiful and complex to contemplate: beautiful due to the synchronization, homogeneity, and unity described in this type of motion, and complex because there are many parameters to be handled in order to evoke these characteristics. According to Fruin (1971b, c) crowd behavior is affected by the spatial perception of each individual considering her own knowledge and intelligence. When the environment is known, the individual can make a decision based also on social and cultural patterns. Personal preferences also affect how close people can get to each other. The space occupied by people and their relationships with others was studied by Edward Hall (1966). According to this American anthropologist, who coined the term Proxemics, each person has a set of nested spaces around the body: public, social, personal, and intimate. The personal space can vary based on the kinds of interaction and relationships of the people involved. In addition, the interpersonal distance among people in crowds can also be affected by individual characteristics such as gender, age of each individual, and her physical state.

We know that some places can be propitious to crowd formation. Such places can include airports, train stations, and public areas, for example. The existence of places propitious for crowd formation, leads governments, managers, researchers, designers, and other professionals to be acutely interested in the development of technologies to improve the security and comfort of those places. One of these relatively new technologies is computational crowd simulation.

Crowd Simulation addresses related problems in the entertainment (games and movies) and safety industries. For entertainment, we can easily apply crowd simulation to populate scenes of a game or movie with realistic and dynamic crowds, e.g., during simulated warfare, or by audience enhancement to reduce the expense of human extras. On the other hand, in safety engineering, avoidance of injury is the primary concern, and we can observe some open research problems when crowds are considered. In this book, we show the state of the art in this area and also point out open problems and proposed solutions. Indeed, our focus is to discuss evacuation models, the importance of evaluation, and validation in these situations and case studies, e.g., games at stadiums, public buildings, train stations, etc. Such understanding allows engineers to design better places and also to figure out the best way to guide people when choosing an evacuation route.

Various approaches have been proposed in the literature over the last few decades motivating the development of different scientific crowd motion models. Such approaches are concerned with computational simulation of individual motion behavior, small groups, and crowds. These models were designed based on different goals and complexity levels. The first known model is a local rules-based system (Reynolds 1987) able to simulate the behavior of flocks, herds, and schools of animal surrogates called "boids", where all individuals are homogeneous with respect to their rule parameters. An important and current aspect in simulated crowd behavior is that individual parameters characterize heterogeneous crowds, where decisions and actions can vary from one to another and differently influence crowd evolution. Some recent publications discuss the importance of having heterogeneous agents in a crowd (Pelechano et al. 2016). Also, navigation and steering behaviors have achieved increasingly realistic results, (Patil et al. 2011; Berseth et al. 2015a; Boatright et al. 2014).

Despite these recent developments, there are still open opportunities to consider the simulation process for emergency situations and application of methods in real life. This book aims to discuss some of these aspects, and it is organized as follows. First, we discuss some theory and methods behind crowd simulation, crowd dynamics and evolution in egress situations, and regulations in evacuation processes which can vary from place to place in the world. Then, we focus on crowd simulation technologies describing some current extant possibilities for people who want to work or develop tools in the area. In Chap. 3 we present CrowdSim, the software developed by the authors. We also discuss the challenging problem of validation and comparison of simulation with real-life situations. In Chap. 4 the CrowdSim software is the basis for several case study scenarios drawn from real-life applications. Finally, in Chap. 5 we discuss the prospect of performing crowd motion analysis using computer vision techniques.

Chapter 2
Background Review

This chapter introduces some important aspects of crowd dynamics and crowd evacuation, and discusses regulations concerning evacuation processes as discussed and presented in some countries.

2.1 Theories in Crowd Research

First of all, we define some concepts related to crowds. A crowd represents a large group of individuals in the same environment. Despite that, its formation can occur voluntarily or non-voluntarily, in everyday situations as well as in specific exceptional cases. This is a simple, but very important, concept that we illustrate in Fig. 2.1: people voluntarily become part of a crowd formed by the audience of a music festival (a). On the other hand, an involuntary crowd emerged during the motion of people in a train station (b). Furthermore, we can also highlight, i.e., panic or emergency situations as a trigger for crowd formation, like the evacuation process surrounding the 9/11 events in New York City.

In order to identify a large group of people as a crowd, some criteria are expected to be observed. Challenger (2009) highlights some of them:

- *Size*: There should be a measurable gathering of people.
- *Density*: Crowd members should be colocated in a particular area, with a sufficient density distribution.
- *Time*: Individuals should typically come together in a specific location for a specific purpose over a measurable amount of time.
- *Collectivity*: Crowd members should share a social identity, common goals, and interests, and act in a coherent manner.
- *Novelty*: Individuals should be able to act in a socially coherent manner, despite coming together in an ambiguous or unfamiliar situation.

© Springer International Publishing AG 2017
V.J. Cassol et al., *Simulating Crowds in Egress Scenarios*,
https://doi.org/10.1007/978-3-319-65202-3_2

(a)   (b)

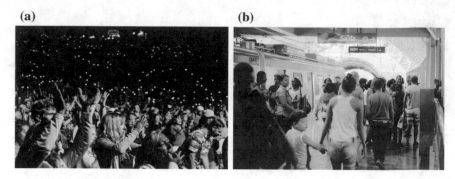

Fig. 2.1 Two different examples of crowds which have emerged in different circumstances: a music festival (**a**) and a train station (**b**). "Ververidis Vasilis/www.Shutterstock.com"

As different events and circumstances can set the stage for crowd formation, some researchers have tried to categorize the different types of crowds. There is no one typical crowd, but a range of crowd types, each with their own characteristics and typical behaviors. Berlonghi (1995-02-01T00:00:00), in 1995, identified five different types of crowds. In order to illustrate each types, we searched the Internet for illustrative examples, shown in Fig. 2.2:

- *Spectator*: A crowd watching an event that they have come to the location to see, or that they happen to discover once there (Fig. 2.2a).
- *Demonstrator*: A crowd, often with a recognized leader, organized for a specific reason or event, to picket, demonstrate, march, or chant (Fig. 2.2b).
- *Dense or Suffocating*: A crowd in which the free movement of people decreases quickly and sometimes can stop. Due to high crowd density, people may be swept along and compressed, resulting in serious injuries and fatalities from suffocation (Fig. 2.2c).
- *Violent*: A crowd attacking, terrorizing, or rioting with no consideration for the law or the rights of other people (Fig. 2.2d).
- *Escaping*: A crowd attempting to escape from real or perceived danger or life-threatening situations, including people involved in organized evacuations, or chaotic pushing and shoving by a panicking mob (Fig. 2.2e).

Our goal is to study the attributes that characterize crowd dynamics in order to understand how crowds are likely to move and behave.

2.1.1 Crowd Dynamics

The observation of crowd evolution in a specific place allows us to observe different aspects. A crowd consists of independent individuals and each one has her own needs and desires, but all of them share the same goal. Such a group feeling is highlighted

Fig. 2.2 The five types of crowds according to Berlonghi (1995-02-01T00:00:00): spectator (**a**), demonstrator (**b**), dense or suffocating (**c**), violent (**d**), and escaping (**e**)

by Osorio (2003), a psychologist, who defines a crowd of people as a human system composed of a set of people able to know each other as individuals, yet share goals and perform a collective action.

The understanding of human behavior is a huge research field in psychology area reaching back into the 1800s. By the beginning of twentieth century, Freud already had spent decades observing human behavior Freud (1922). Supported by studies from LeBon (1895) and Mc Dougall (2009), Freud discusses the behavior of human beings when part of a group and defines a crowd as a temporary entity, consisting of heterogeneous elements that have joined together for a moment.

Other crowd aspects were observed and described by the end of the nineteenth century. One of them was observed by LeBon (1895), who says that when part of a crowd, individuals can perform unusual behaviors which they are not liable to perform alone. In this kind of situation, the individuals can act in collectively and emerge as a new entity. This new entity can make people feel, think, and act in different ways, even being able to perform dangerous behaviors which can result in fatalities.

We know that a crowd is a congregation of people in the same environment, yet every individual in a crowd is owner of his or her own personal space in the environment. The American anthropologist Edward Hall invented the term *proxemics* Hall (1966) to represent the personal space of each person. Hall noted that the distance between people, when interacting with each other, varies according to their relationship, or level of intimacy. These levels are divided in four possible ranges (see Fig. 2.3): *intimate* [0.00, 0.45] m, *personal* (0.45, 1.20] m, *social* (1.20, 3.60] m, and *public* (3.60, 7.60] m.

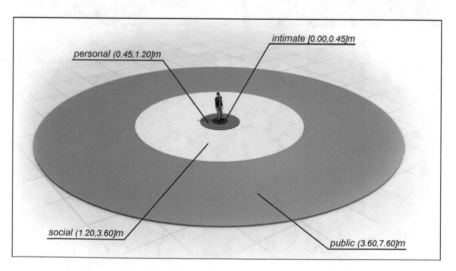

Fig. 2.3 Illustration of a person's proxemics based on Hall's definitions of distances: intimate, personal, social, and public

Knowing the proxemics of the individuals in a group may make it possible to identify the groups' relationship into the crowd Edney and Grundmann (1979). Such aspect is considered because groups of people can perform different behaviors based on its size, place, or even the relationship among the group members.

Still (2000) developed a set of computer programs in order to study, and also reproduce, the behavior of a crowd. His framework, called *Legion*, was based on four rules to determine the flow of human traffic. These rules interact as characters come into proximity with each other's space and associated static and dynamic objects in the environment. The computational result exhibits emergent behavior, specifically, the entities are programmed with one kind of behavior but the group of entities exhibits another, more global, property. Where the group behavior cannot be reduced to the individuals' behavior, a system is defined as emergent (Fig. 2.4).

Still's simulation research focused interest in emergent behaviors from real crowds. These group attributes were observed by other authors Helbing and Molnar (1998) and recognized by international institutions Challenger (2009). Computational crowd simulation should reproduce these behaviors when possible:

(a) Arch Formation   (b) Lane Formation

(c) Corner Effect   (d) Ring Effect

Fig. 2.4 Crowd organization examples

- *Arch Formation*: Arching happens when a large, dense crowd pushes forward toward a narrow exit. In situations like this, the exit becomes clogged and the crowd forms an arch-like shape in front of the exit.
- *Lane Formation*: When people move in the same or opposing directions, they can self-organize to create distinct lanes: one for each direction of movement, or sometimes differentiating by velocities. This self-organization phenomena helps to reduce collisions and increase the lane's overall speed. However, in high density or nervous crowds, any lanes formed may break down due to continuous overtaking maneuvers.
- *Corner Effect*: As crowd members turn corners, they tend to slow down and move further into the corner, becoming more densely packed and appearing to *hug* the corner.
- *Ring Effect*: This phenomena emerges when a crowd is observing a particular event or gathers around a particular point of interest, such as a street artist. In such cases a ring structure emerges, radiating outwards from the point of interest.
- *Speed reduction effect*: This effect arises when many people are populating a specific environment and moving in some direction. If more people arrive, the crowd velocity may decrease.
- *Principle of Least Effort*: When possible, crowd members will typically take the fastest route. They aim to minimize time and work, avoid congestion, and maximize their speed.

Having just described some important aspects related to crowds in general, the next section can now specify some aspects observed in crowds during an egress event.

2.1.2 Crowd Evolution in Egress Situations

As observed by LeBon (1895), when in crowds, people can perform unusual behaviors which can lead to irrational actions. Indeed, we can say that such actions can occur even more likely under panicked egress. It is very easy to look back in history to point out some important involuntary evacuation situations:

1. Atomic bombing of Japan during World War II;
2. Terrorists reach New York in 2001;
3. Hurricane Katrina in 2005.

These are just three examples where evacuations were needed. In such situations, people probably were guided by their simple emotions and responded to the situation performing unusual behavior.

The success of an evacuation event can be related to an understanding of the process. In order to have a safe evacuation there are three important factors: interpretation, preparation, and action Mu et al. (2013). *Interpretation* is the moment when people perceive the real need to evacuate; *preparation* is planning the best route to follow, while *action* guides the individual through the chosen route in order to reach a safe area.

In addition, other specific aspects influence evacuation success, including:

- Building type, such as, office, airport, train station;
- The understanding of occupants' behavior under panic situation;
- Occupants' distribution (by age, gender, and disability); and
- Location of dangerous areas as well as safe places and emergency exits.

Knowledge about such aspects facilitates the execution of a safe egress process. The evolution of a crowd during an evacuation process usually shows behaviors that can evidence the organization and structure of the group. A successful egress is often due to cooperation and coordination among the people Cocking and Drury (2008).

Usually, the group has power to influence its members' motion. Thus the choice of escape route, *made individually*, usually is also influenced by the actions of the other members of the crowd. This aspect can justify the fact that when in egress, people typically move in the same direction as others. In this way, for Cocking and Drury (2008), when united by an emergency situation, a physical crowd (a group of individuals in the same location, each with her own personal identity) may be transformed into a psychological crowd (i.e., a group of people united by a common social identity as members of a particular category).

Additionally other factors (mapped by Challenger (2009)) may influence an evacuation process:

- *Mobility*: An individual who is less mobile is likely to need longer to evacuate in an emergency.
- *Physical Position*: An individual lying down is likely to have a slower rate of reaction and movement than an individual standing up.
- *Density*: Crowd movement will be slower in a more densely packed environment.
- *Alertness*: An individual who is less alert, for instance as a result of tiredness or intoxication, is likely to react more slowly in the event of an emergency.
- *Visibility*: The more visible the signage and emergency exit routes, the more attractive they are likely to be to crowd members and the more likely (and at higher speed) crowd members are to follow those routes.
- *Complexity of the environment*: The more complex the environment, the more indecisive individuals are likely to be and the longer it is likely to take to evacuate.

These factors are usually considered in order to regulate any egress process. Government groups and different professional organizations have worked in regulate egress features and protocols. The next section presents and details some of these regulations.

2.2   Regulations in Evacuation Processes

Nowadays, governments and professionals from different fields work together to define and specify effective measures for optimal evacuation plans. The purpose of an evacuation plan is to guarantee safety when leaving a building or structure, specially when a panic or an emergency situation occurs. An evaluation of egress details is already requested by international organizations as UEFA (Union of European Football Association) or FIFA (Fédération Internationale de Football Association) in specific sites as sport stadiums and arenas, beyond specific regional regulations.

The UEFA expresses specific concerns related to egress processing which must be observed even before the design of a new stadium starts Fenwick et al. (2011). The safe capacity is a mandatory requirement which focuses, as the name suggests, on ensuring maximum safety for spectators. It is widely accepted that all spectators should be able to exit the stadium bowl to a point of safety within a maximum of eight minutes. This value is based on a maximum flow rate through the stadiums exits of 660 people an hour. However, there may be some consideration for specific variations based on the size and design of the venue.

According to FIFA, the emergency evacuation time is in part based on the level of risk and the available emergency evacuation routes to places of safety or places of reasonable safety. The organization has published a guideline[1] where they define a set of Stadium Safety and Security Regulations. According to this guide, factors like the type of construction and materials used in the stadium will have an impact on the calculation of the expected time for evacuation. In addition, fire is one of the major risks to be considered when calculating the acceptable egress time. For example, if the risk of fire is high due to the construction of the stadium, the expected evacuation time must be reduced.

The emergency evacuation time is not a fixed value. It is a calculation which, together with the appropriate rate of passage, is used to determine the capacity of the emergency exit system from the viewing accommodation to a place of safety or reasonable safety, during an emergency.

The United States of America considers the *Life Safety Code* (2015), a guideline developed by the NFPA (National Fire Protection Association), which provides details to be followed during a possible building evacuation process. Together with the *Design Handbook* provided by the SFPE (Society of Fire Protection and Engineering) Hurley et al. (2015), building designers can incorporate, during the project phase of a building, egress aspects regarding to features such as sprinklers, exit lights, and alarms.

According to the *International Building Code* International Code Council (2012), every building or structure, new or old, designed for human occupancy, is to be provided with exits sufficient to permit the prompt escape of occupants in case of fire or other emergency. According to the guideline, all exits should discharge directly

---

[1]http://fifa.com/mm/document/tournament/competition/51/53/98/safetyregulations_e.pdf.

to the street or other open space that gives safe access to a public way. The streets to which the exits discharge must be of a width adequate to accommodate all persons leaving the building. An EAP (*emergency action plan*), according to the guideline, should cover those designated actions that ensure occupant safety from fire and other emergencies:

- Emergency escape procedures and emergency escape route assignments;
- Procedures to account for all individuals after emergency evacuation has been completed;
- The preferred means of reporting fires and other emergencies; and
- Names or regular job titles of persons or departments who can be contacted for further information or explanation of duties under the plan.

Independent of the guideline, it is important to mention that personal behavior can contribute to some emergency or congestion that is not predicted during the egress plan development.

Legislation on crowd management in Brazil is under development, having been given increased attention in the past few years due to some specific events. One motivation has been the unfortunate fatal disaster in the Kiss Night Club.[2] In addition, big sportive events that took place in Brazil (the World Cup and the Olympics) are helping to promote the new legislation.

The ABNT (Brazilian Association of Technical Standards) defined in 2001 the guideline NBR 9077:2001 aiming to specify regulations concerning emergency exits. According to the guideline, the concentration of people when using an emergency exit should be maximum $2 people/m^2$. The Technical Guideline from the government of São Paulo, Brazil Polícia Militar do Estado de São Paulo (2004), defines specific points relating to safety during egress. We summarize some of the most important:

- Individuals should achieve a safe point without walking more than 20 m in outdoor areas and 10 m in indoor areas. Emergency exits can be considered as the safe point.
- The time for a group of people to leave a public indoor area, such as a theater, should not exceed 6 min.
- The concentration of people in stand-up areas should not be greater than $4 people/m^2$.

We opted to present data From São Paulo due the fact the city is considered the most important city in Brazil. Each state or city can provide their own building regulations, in the absence of operative federal regulations.

---

[2]http://edition.cnn.com/2013/01/28/world/americas/brazil-nightclub-fire.

2.3   Crowd Simulation in Emergency Situations

An important work regarding crowd behavior in egress situations was proposed by
Braun et al. (2003). The authors explore the agents' personal characteristics in order
to simulate different reactions and behaviors during an evacuation process. Inspired
by a physically based approach Helbing et al. (2000), the authors aggregate a set of
features to simulate agents and also groups in order to reproduce a heterogeneous
crowd. Such features include, among others, aspects such as families representation,
dependency level from others, level of agent's altruism, and also desired velocity.
The authors keep groups together considering a force composed from the altruism
level from agents of the same family. In addition, based on the altruism level, an
agent can ungroup from her family in order to help other agents in the process.

The work from ZHU et al. (2008) was developed observing the 2008 Olympic
games in China. At that time, the authors developed an approach able to reproduce
pedestrian traffic created from delegations of athletes from different countries and
also the audience. A case study was performed considering the *National Stadium* and
took into account aspects such as the number of pedestrians and their distribution
during specific situations (such the final moments of a game).

The main goal envisaged by Fu et al. (2014) was to simulate the normal evacuation
process. Their motivation was to reproduce pedestrian behavior in exit selection
taking into account a least effort cellular automaton algorithm. Space is represented
by a set of 2D cells containing pedestrians or obstacles. The motions and goals used
to guide the movements are defined considering a probabilistic approach. Cellular
automaton algorithms are used by Ji et al. (2013) for pedestrian dynamics and by Aik
and Choon (2012) for reproducing a simple evacuation process. Chu et al. (2014)
developed the platform SAFEgress (Social Agent For Egress), in which building
occupants are modeled as agents able to choose their actions according to their
knowledge of the environment and their interactions with the social groups and
the neighboring crowd. According to the authors, results show that both the agents'
familiarity with the building and social influences can significantly impact evacuation
performance.

Pelechano et al. (2008) have explored different aspects of virtual crowd behaviors.
One aspect they studied involved improving a crowd simulation by adding a psychological model Pelechano et al. (2005). A more extensive framework combines
PMFserv Silverman et al. (2006) (mature models for physiology, stress, perception, and emotion) with the Multi-Agent Communication for Evacuation Simulation
(MACES) system Pelechano and Badler (2006). The integration allowed the crowd
simulation model to provide events that an agent can perceive, resulting in responsive,
reactive, and situated behaviors.

A review of crowd simulation models and selected commercial software tools for
high-rise building evacuation was developed by Pelechano and Malkawi (2008). The
goal of that work was to study the importance of incorporating human psychological
and physiological factors into crowd simulation models. The authors presented an
overview of fundamentals that should be applied to simulate human movement to

align it closer to real movements of people, where interaction between bodies emerges and flow rates, densities, and speeds become the result of those interactions instead of some predefined values.

Besides agents and environment, some external factors can influence the results of a simulation. Such external factors can include, not exclusively, aspects of fire and smoke propagation, e.g., as discussed by Huang et al. (2010). The authors developed MIMOSA (Mine Interior Model Of Smoke and Action), which integrates an underground coal mine virtual environment, a fire and smoke propagation model, and a human physiology and behavior model. The authors consider the particular effects of smoke and toxic fumes on the agents in the simulation. To accomplish this, each individual agent has a set of physiological parameters dependent on its local environment, simulating a miner's physiological exposure and consequent condition during normal operations as well as during emergencies due to fire and smoke.

Xi and Smith (2015) developed a virtual fire evacuation training system. Their idea was focused on extending a virtual environment development pipeline for building virtual fire evacuation training systems. The authors investigate the best way to integrate 3D building models and fire egress behavior from fire evacuation simulations into a game engine. The aim is to ensure that the behavior of autonomous agents, representing human evacuees extracted from the fire simulator, is faithfully represented in the target virtual environment. A pipeline is presented as example to show the integration of Google SketchUp,[3] FDS+Evac Korhonen et al. (2009) and Unity 3D.[4]

Beyond the analyses of agents' behaviors, it is very important to consider the way environment can contribute (or not) to a possible egress process. This is one of the goals considered in research developed by Berseth et al. (2015b), who observe how the layout of a building affects the flow patterns of its intended users. The authors propose a computational framework for studying the configuration of architectural building elements. Such elements can represent pillars or doors and are studied in order to optimize dense pedestrian flow during building evacuations. One of the aspects considered by the authors was the effect of local collision avoidance strategies used in crowd flow patterns on representative evacuation benchmarks. The benchmarks include variations in the number and placement of pillars, exit door sizes, as well as corridor and crowd flow configurations. Three different steering algorithms (ORCA van den Berg et al. (2009), PPR Singh et al. (2011), and SF Helbing et al. (2000)) were applied in order to observe the resulting optimizations. According to the authors, when the main goal is to study real buildings, it is important to provide approaches validated with the local population. In addition, they conclude that door widths are an important design feature. Door widths had a significant impact on crowd flow patterns, especially for bidirectional traffic, highlighting the importance of selecting the right door width based on the expected crowd interactions.

Also regarding the environment structure, the work presented by Jiang et al. aims to increase environment safety by analyzing better placement of obstacles Jiang et al.

---

[3]http://sketchup.com.
[4]http://unity3d.com.

(2014). In order to reach this goal, the authors developed a genetic algorithm based on social-forces. According to them, simulation results indicate that appropriately placing two pillars on both sides but not in front of a door can maximize escape efficiency. In order to validate results, they performed an experiment using 80 participants. Results indicated that human actions corresponded well with the simulations.

Motion information is also considered by Rodriguez et al. (2013), who investigate the use of tools from robotics control to improve the design of buildings. The authors apply methods of optimization and roadmap-based motion planning to determine how placement of agents and common design features, such as pillars and doors, can affect the flow of human traffic through a building. Some experiments had objectives to explore pedestrian flow rate optimization via pillar placement, evacuation time via door placement, and the optimization of agent meeting points.

After having defined an ideal environment, it is also interesting to define the ideal parameters for possible steering algorithms. This aspect is also discussed by Berseth and collaborators Berseth et al. (2014). The authors present a methodology for automatically fitting the parameters of a steering algorithm. The goal is to minimize any combination of performance metrics, across any set of environment benchmarks in a general, model-independent fashion. Named *SteerFit*, the framework can optimize steering algorithms according to different criteria: distance, time, or energy consumption of an agent, its computational performance, similarity to ground truth, user-defined custom metrics, or a weighted combination of any of them. The framework was applied in order to fit parameters for three steering algorithms: ORCA van den Berg et al. (2009), PPR Singh et al. (2011) and SF Helbing et al. (2000). According to the authors, the parameter fitting can be used to improve the performance of a specific algorithm. The optimization also can be considered as an analysis tool able to produce a detailed view of an algorithm's behavior relative to its internal parameters.

Beyond the simulation of one egress path, it is interesting to observe different ways that people leave an environment. One alternative for egress plan generation is the use of matheuristic, which decomposes the problem being solved into a master and a set of subproblems. The work of Pillac et al. (2014) presents an evacuation algorithm that follows recommended evacuation methodologies, which divides the evacuated area in evacuation zones, each being instructed to leave at a specific time and following a predefined route. According to the authors, the *Conflict-Based Path-Generation Heuristic* specifies evacuation routes for each evacuation zone and uses a lexicographic objective function that first maximizes the number of evacuees reaching safety and then minimizes the total evacuation time. The algorithm was evaluated taking into account real-scale, massive flood scenarios in the Hawkesbury-Nepean River, Australia. The simulation considered 70,000 agents who required evacuation from the area.

One of the main points to be considered when simulating crowds is the validation of results. The best strategy, in this case, is to compare data from simulation with real-life experience. Chapter 5 discusses many techniques currently used to extract data from crowds in video sequences that can be used to this end. One work in the area is by Murphy et al. (2013): they present EvacSim, a multi-agent building evacuation simulation. Here, the authors detail pedestrian model elements that govern microscopic agent movement such as personal space preservation, obstacle avoidance, and moving together as a crowd. In order to validate the EvacSim pedestrian model against real-world pedestrian data, the authors made a comparison of flow rates, density, and velocity for corridor entry and for merging groups, considering data from simulation and the real world in a controlled environment.

Guy et al. (2012) developed a statistical similarity measure for aggregate crowd dynamics. The method aims to measure the similarity between a given set of observed, real-world data and a visual simulation technique for aggregate crowd motions of many individual agents. This metric uses a two-step process to quantify a simulator's ability to reproduce the collective behaviors of the whole system, as observed in the recorded real-world data. Wang et al. (2016) propose a new approach based on finding latent path patterns in both real and simulated data in order to analyze and compare them. Unsupervised clustering by nonparametric Bayesian inference is used to learn the patterns, which themselves provide a rich visualization of the crowd's behavior. To this end, they present a new Stochastic Variational Dual Hierarchical Dirichlet Process (SV-DHDP) model. The fidelity of the patterns is then computed with respect to a reference, thus allowing the outputs of different algorithms to be compared with each other or with real data.

2.4 Summary

This chapter presented a literature analysis regarding theories of crowd dynamics and evolution, and further discussed the regulation of egress situations in different countries. In addition, we presented the state of the art in crowd evacuation techniques. The next Chapter presents current crowd simulation technologies, including some commercially distributed, and CrowdSim, which is the software used in Chap. 4 to explain and discuss case-studies.

Chapter 3
Crowd Simulation

This chapter presents some current technologies in crowd simulation and it is organized into two parts. First, we present and discuss the main existing state-of-the-art technologies developed with an explicit goal to simulate crowds. Then we present in detail CrowdSim, a new crowd simulation software developed by the authors. This is not a commercial software, however it has been used in many real-life cases, so we can present some performed experiments and our experiences with it in Chap. 4.

3.1 Existing Technologies

Crowd management is widely applied with the goal of providing important information about potential human behavior. One of the major strategies to ensure audience safety is by practicing effective crowd management strategies.

In the United States, one of the most important challenges facing police executives is the need to prepare their departments for major events control. They have published a report which explores some of the key issues that have proved important or difficult in the real world of major events management (Police Executive Research Forum 2011). This kind of management helps event organizers identify agglomeration areas, bottleneck regions, as well as attention points and other situations. Nowadays, important events are supported by crowd management teams.

One component of crowd management is egress. Egress problems can be observed in different types of systems, such as buildings, cities, or transportation. The use of simulation software allows safety engineers to validate, explore, and also predict crowd behavior in a specific building or outside environment without the need to utilize real people. In addition, such possibilities are even more important when simulating a building during its design phase by identifying improvement and attention points in ample time to be fixed. It is possible to identify several positive points about commercial software used to produce crowd simulations, for example:

© Springer International Publishing AG 2017
V.J. Cassol et al., *Simulating Crowds in Egress Scenarios*,
https://doi.org/10.1007/978-3-319-65202-3_3

Fig. 3.1 Illustrations from VSTEP—Crowd Control Trainer

- To reproduce exact desired scenarios, including panic situations which are difficult to be performed safely by actual people.
- To visualize any possible crowd-related incident and improve preparedness;
- To avoid the high training costs of practical training; and
- To learn the necessary skills to be acquired and applied in a realistic environment.

In order to produce realistic results and to predict crowd behaviors aimed toward alerting events managers, some commercial software systems are currently used by crowd management teams in different countries. The next sections describe several important commercial crowd simulators.

3.1.1 Crowd Control Trainer

Crowd Control Trainer is a simulator solution to train people who work with crowd-related incidents and mass events. The software was developed by VSTEP,[1] an ISO9001:2008[2] certified company, in cooperation with the Rotterdam Police and the Dutch Government. This partnership was formed in order to support their police commanders and crowd control training managers. In addition, the software was selected by the government of The Netherlands as one of the best in the field of safety and security enhancement.

The simulation takes place in a realistic virtual 3D replica of the actual urban environment allowing instant recognition and realistic planning of an actual management and response strategy for demonstrations and riots. The software includes movement and AI algorithms in order to compute motion of crowds of any size through the virtual training environment. Some different views of results provided by the software are illustrated in Fig. 3.1.

Furthermore, the *Crowd Control Trainer* allows the police commanders to train in guiding crowds and demonstrations. Commanders can close off roads, place different kinds of barriers in the environment, and instantly witness the effect these decisions have on the crowd movement. To prevent mass events from getting out of hand, the

---

[1] http://vstepsimulation.com.
[2] http://iso.org/iso/catalogue_detail?csnumber=46486.

(a) Toronto - Union Station   (b) JFK - Terminal Five   (c) San Francisco - Train
                                                                  Station

Fig. 3.2 Illustration of results from *MassMotion* projects: Union Station in Toronto (**a**), JFK Airport
(**b**) and San Francisco Train Station (**c**)

Crowd Control Trainer allows simulation and training of riot prevention strategies.
Commanders can introduce special police forces, vehicles, and mounted police into
the scenario in an attempt to restore and maintain order and instantly see the effects
their actions have on crowd movement and behavior.

3.1.2 MassMotion

MassMotion, developed by *Oasys Software*,[3] is designed for the creation and execution of large-scale 3D crowd simulations. The company has worked on *MassMotion*
for the past 10 years. The software started as a pedestrian movement simulator and
has evolved into an evacuation package.

The simulator operates on a full 3D model environment. Each individual agent
is made aware of their environment through bitmap representations of free and
obstructed space on all walkable areas. Each agent determines their best available
target location for the next frame of the simulation and adjusts their velocity and orientation to achieve that position. This calculation is executed at a rate of five frames
per second of simulated time, which is frequent enough to allow agents to adjust
to dynamically changing conditions within the environment without encroaching on
locations occupied by obstructions or other agents.

The simulation is based on academic research, supported by observed crowd
behavior, and rendered with gaming-quality graphics. Figure 3.2 illustrates visualization provided by *MassMotion* for different projects.

MassMotion also contains an analysis tool which permits the examination, after
simulations, of how long it took people to get from one point to another, the flow
rates for doors, stairs, and escalators, and the comfort rating in different parts of
the model and at various times. This information is presented in graphs and visual
representations.

Among the applications for *MassMotion*, the company suggests:

---

[3]http://oasys-software.com.

- **Airport Terminal Design**: Including curbside with vehicles, passenger movement and processing, baggage handling, and ground side operations modeling;
- **Rail and Transit**: Large, high density crowds, and schedule-based activity, and neighborhood dispersion including road crossings.
- **District Modeling**: Significant scalability which enables the simulation of urban areas; and
- **Fire and Evacuation**: Multi-floor evacuation by stairs and elevators.

3.1.3 Legion

Legion's simulation products,[4] developed in the United Kingdom, include a set of tools able to deal with pedestrian behaviors. *Legion-Evac* is an agent-based simulation tool where each agent can move in the environment, from an origin to a destination, weaving through the crowd and performing various activities and behaviors along its journey. Agents make decisions in the environment according to the principle of least effort. In addition, random elements that influence behavior can be introduced to make the simulation more realistic, e.g., entity size, speed, age, and luggage.

The software's crowd simulation can be used to assist projects with different goals, most importantly:

- *Building Design*: Validate all spaces used by people;
- *Operations*: Design optimal procedures for crowd event venues;
- *Strategic Planning*: Evaluate costs and benefits of major capital projects prior to implementation;
- *Safety and Security*: Design, test, and improve evacuation procedures; and
- *3D visualizations*: Demonstrate visually how a scheme would function in reality.

The company has recently undertaken projects for different customers[5] (Fig. 3.3 illustrates some of them). One notable *Legion* project was developed with the goal of simulating Olympic sites. In 2000, the Sydney Organizing Committee for the Olympic Games used *Legion* software to assess pedestrian circulation through the Olympic Park. Simulations identified, among other points, unacceptably high congestion at a crucial juncture of Olympic Boulevard which prompted modifications to the design of Olympic Park. *Legion* has also apparently developed crowd simulation projects for all subsequent Olympics games through at least 2012.

Another option offered by *Legion* is the animation of realistic pedestrians and crowd movement within a 3D environment.[6] The service takes a designer's 3D model of a building or urban environment and then adds realistic animated crowds. An illustration of this facility is presented in Fig. 3.4. Whether there are two or 20,000

---

[4]http://legion.com.

[5]http://legion.com/case-studies.

[6]http://www.legion.com/news/legion-launches-3d-crowd-animation-service.

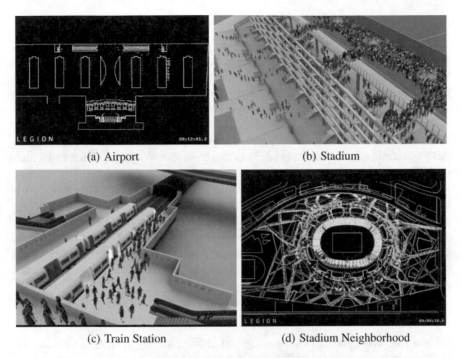

(a) Airport   (b) Stadium

(c) Train Station   (d) Stadium Neighborhood

Fig. 3.3 Illustrations of Legion simulations: airport (**a**), stadium (**b**), train station (**c**), and stadium neighborhood (**d**)

Fig. 3.4 Illustration of 3D Crowd Animation Service from Legion

people moving through a scene, it gives clients, the public, and planners a better understanding of how a proposed development will be used and the impact it will have on human behaviors.

3.1.4   Massive

Massive software[7] was initially developed to perform crowd simulation for "The Lord Of The Rings" film trilogy. In 2004, the founder and director of *Massive*, Stephen Regelous, received a Scientific and Engineering Achievement Academy Award for the design and development of *Massive*. The software was designed applying AI-driven autonomous agents in order to generate character animation. The crowd and battle scenes produced by *Massive* are an important aspect in the field of animation production and can be observed in different animation movies as reported by Kaniuk (2017).

According to the *Massive* company, one key feature of its product is that it employs an "Artificial Life" approach to AI. Artificial Life technology draws from the processes of nature rather than traditional simulation methodologies, providing for more inherently natural behavior than those seen in existing engineering solutions. *Massive* agents act individually using simulated natural senses of sight, hearing, and touch. The visualization produced by *Massive* is able to produce dynamic scenes with vehicles as well as people.

The software has been employed by different fields, in varying projects, for very significant brands; for example:

- **Film Industry**: The software was applied in film industry in order to produce AI-driven character animation. The first and most famous *Massive* projects were the battle scenes of the "Lord of the Rings" trilogy. Movie effects companies which have employed *Massive* software in their projects include Pixar,[8] Sony Pictures Imageworks,[9] Rhythm & Hues,[10] Digital Domain,[11] Framestore CFC,[12] and The Mill[13];
- **Television and Games**: *Massive*âÂŹs products are employed in games to populate *cutscenes* with large, realistic, and dynamic crowds. High-profile game studios using *Massive* can be found throughout Asia and North America, and these projects have been featured on both the XBOX 360 and Nintendo Wii platforms. The same application can be found in TV productions, such as "Game of Thrones";
- **Architectural Visualization**: *Massive* is applied to provide virtual environments populated with photorealistic moving people; and
- **Engineering Simulation**: *Massive*'s simulations are employed in civil engineering, pedestrian planning, and transportation.

---

[7] http://massivesoftware.com.

[8] http://pixar.com.

[9] http://imageworks.com.

[10] http://rhythm.com.

[11] http://digitaldomain.com.

[12] http://framestore.com.

[13] http://themill.com.

3.1.5 Golaem

Golaem[14] is a plugin for Maya[15] able to populate 3D scenes. The population can include, not exclusively, humans, horses, birds, or other creatures. In order to create more realistic scenes, the software provides simulations taking into account aspects such as animation and behavioral variations.

Golaem is used in the production of well-known movies and TV shows, e.g., Game of Thrones (season 5). When creating a crowd scene, different aspects and situations may be desired. *Golaem* can be employed for different targets (or a mix of them), e.g.,:

- *Audiences*: Stadiums or concert halls can be populated with thousands of fans; in addition, it is possible to generate geometry and shading diversity;
- *City and public spaces*: Traversable spaces may have virtual agents. Such situations may consist of just a few pedestrians in a city street or include the population of a full city. Furthermore, the software is able to detect roads or sidewalks and make the characters navigate on them. Regarding the motion of characters, *Golaem* also determines the best animation motions as the agents follow their trajectories (Fig. 3.5).
- *Battles*: *Golaem* addresses different areas involved in generating a battle scene. Such areas include: agent formations, locomotion on rough terrain, horses, physics simulation, and interaction with other special effects. In order to differentiate the agents involved into a battle, the software applies different methods to simulate clothes.
- *Creatures*: *Golaem* can manipulate creatures other than humans. The set of creatures is huge, including aliens, spiders, rats, insects, birds, fish, and even bikes. The *Golaem* animation engine provides different ground adaptation methods and trajectory computation algorithms in order to deal with such varied populations.

For pathfinding and navigation (Fig. 3.5), considering random and target-based paths, *Golaem* provides several useful features:

- Automatic obstacle detection;
- Collision avoidance with obstacles and other agents; and
- Different crowd formation and flocking behaviors (for birds, fish, etc.).

All parts of the software are coded using MEL or Python. A C/C++ API enables the user to read the exported simulation data.

---

[14]http://golaem.com.
[15]http://autodesk.com/products/maya.

Fig. 3.5 City population and crowd navigation computed by *Golaem*. "Made by Rotor Studios by using Golaem"

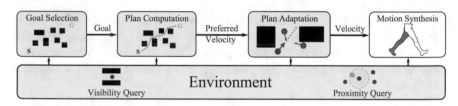

Fig. 3.6 *Menge* subproblems workflow (Curtis et al. 2016)

3.1.6 Menge

Menge[16] is a cross-platform, modular framework for crowd simulation. The software was developed at the University of North Carolina at Chapel Hill[17] by the *Gamma Research Group*.[18]

    Menge concentrates on various aspects of crowd simulation which support research and development of this field. Its architecture is inspired by an implicit decomposition of the problem of simulating crowds into component subproblems. An abstraction of *Menge* workflow organized in subproblems is illustrated in Fig. 3.6: first, a goal is selected; second, a base plan to reach that goal is computed; third, the plan is adapted to local and dynamic conditions; and finally, motion is synthesized to provide visualization of the performed plan. Each subproblem may query the environment to support its computation (Curtis et al. 2016).

---

[16]http://gamma.cs.unc.edu/Menge/.

[17]http://unc.edu.

[18]http://gamma.cs.unc.edu.

Fig. 3.7 "The Walking Dead" virtual crowd generated by *Miarmi*. "Image courtesy of digital frontier vfx of USA (www.digitalfrontierfx.com)"

The framework provides a basis for performing independent research in motion planning, collision avoidance, spatial acceleration, and behavioral modeling, among others. The framework can also be used to compare simulations created by different pedestrian models or global navigation algorithms. *Menge* can provide scalable crowds and simulate group formation. The framework is open source and publicly available at no cost.

3.1.7 Miarmy

Miarmy (read "My Army") is a "human logic engine" Maya plugin for AI and behavioral animation, crowd simulation, creature physical simulation, and rendering. Developed by Basefount,[19] this plugin is able to build a human fuzzy logic network without any programming. *Miarmy* supports a standard production pipeline, HumanIK, and Motion Builder tools, and can be integrated with recognized programming libraries, such as PhysX. Miarmy has been employed by the company Digital Frontier VFX to simulate crowds of zombies to the TV show "The Walking Dead"[20] (see Fig. 3.7). Furthermore, the plugin is also employed in the advertising industry to simulate stadium populations and walking pedestrians in ad productions.

3.1.8 Houdini Crowds

Developed by SideFX,[21] the *Houdini* software is able to generate *procedural-based content* for movies, TV, and games. Its exclusive attention to procedural generation

---

[19]http://basefount.com.

[20]http://amc.com/shows/the-walking-dead.

[21]http://sidefx.com.

distinguishes it from other 3D computer graphics software. The crowd system uses artist-friendly shelf tools along with a packed agent primitive type, a Finite State Machine solver, hardware accelerated display of instanced crowds, controls for crowd layout, steering, collision avoidance, terrain adaptation, motion blending, and look-at targets. *Houdini* has been used in various feature animation productions, including the Disney films "Frozen" and "Zootopia".[22]

3.1.9 LCrowdV

Developed by the Gamma Research Group[23] at the University of North Carolina at Chapel Hill, *LCrowdV* is a procedural framework for generating labeled crowd videos.[24] The labeled videos produced help in training models for crowd understanding, including pedestrian detection and crowd classification. Each video generated in *LCrowdV* contains seven labels, which can be varied as parameters, comprising crowd density, population, lighting conditions, background scene, camera angles, agent personality, and noise level. The authors have used *LCrowdV* to improve the performance of pedestrian detection algorithms with training datasets based on labeled real video.

3.2 CrowdSim

CrowdSim is a rule-based crowd simulation software developed to simulate coherent motion and behaviors in an evacuation (Cassol et al. 2012, 2015). Developed at the Virtual Humans Simulation LAB (VHLab)[25] at the Pontifical Catholic University of Rio Grande do Sul,[26] Brazil (Cassol 2016), the software is also capable of generating data that is used to estimate human comfort and safety in a specific environment. During the design phase of CrowdSim, we endeavored to develop software specifically able to:

- Represent the physical geometry of a building in a 3D environment. Such a representation allows safety engineers to use the software in order to simulate an occupation or evacuation plan sensitive to real building physical constraints (doors, emergency exits, and size of corridors).
- Define the spatial occupation of the population in the environment to reproduce initial conditions for an egress event.

---

[22]http://disney.com.

[23]http://gamma.web.unc.edu/.

[24]http://gamma.cs.unc.edu/LCrowdV/Ernest_ECCVW_2016_final.pdf.

[25]http://www.inf.pucrs.br/~vhlab.

[26]http://pucrs.br.

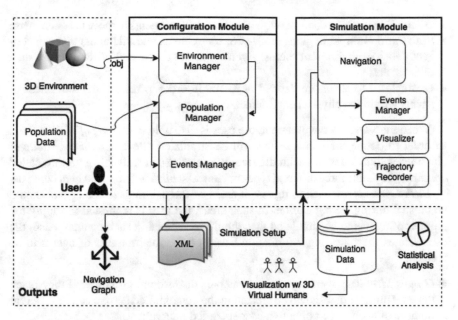

Fig. 3.8 General architecture of CrowdSim

- Model an egress plan in the context of emergency situations triggered by specific events over time: start evacuation, change route, etc.
- Visualize the simulation as an animation as well as summarize relevant data for subsequent statistical analyzes.

Two key components in CrowdSim are organized in distinct modules: *Configuration* and *Simulation*. Figure 3.8 illustrates the software architecture including submodules, the necessary inputs from the user, and produced outputs.

In the following sections we describe the modules of CrowdSim detailing their inputs, dependencies, and workflow.

3.2.1 Setup and Simulation

The configuration module requests, as a first input, the 3D representation of the environment that will be simulated. Such a 3D model will be considered by the *Environment Manager* in order to allow the user to define the walkable regions according to the building structure as well as physical restrictions and obstacles. More specifically, the geometry components can be detailed as follows:

- **Contexts**: Regions (convex or non-convex quadrilaterals) in which agents can be created, move, or be removed. Regions can be classified as birth, moving, or goal, as elaborated later;

- **Doors**: Edges which connect two contexts and allow agents to move between them;
- **Stairs and Ramps**: Regions (convex or non-convex quadrilaterals) that can connect doors from different rooms. Agents can not be created or removed in such regions; and
- **Obstacles**: Obstacles are defined in rooms in order to restrict the movement of agents within the physical environment.

When mapping the environment, the user is also able to define *population data*. In order to define the scenario that will be simulated, the *Environment Manager* classifies walkable regions with different purposes. Such walkable areas are called *contexts*. We define three different types of contexts: *birth*, *motion*, and *goal* contexts.

Birth Contexts are used to represent areas of the building, where agents should be created during the simulation. In such areas, the user is requested to supply the number of agents to be simulated that should be created in such context. Also, the user defines the following information based on the total number of agents to be created:

- *Groups Size*: The agents are created as part of different groups until they reach the total number that should be created in the context. Each group can be different number of agents according to a user-specified interval;
- *Creation Time*: Time that groups of agents start to be created after the beginning of the simulation;
- *Time among groups*: Interval of time to be taken into account when creating different groups. The interval of time make the agents physical distribution not uniform;
- *Goal*: The context (or set of possible contexts) to be considered as goals to be reached by an agent when moving.

Goal Contexts are regions of interest to be considered during agent motion (goals). When creating a goal context, the user is requested to define the percentage of agents that should be removed from the simulation when achieving the context, the percentage of agents that should stay moving in such a context, and the percentage of agents that should find another goal and move in that new direction.

The *Motion Contexts* are considered by the simulation algorithm as connection regions between birth and goal contexts. They are used when calculating an agent's motion route. In addition, a connection graph is built as an output of the configuration module according to connections among contexts and their population specifications. Such contexts allow us to reproduce a virtual environment, as illustrated in Fig. 3.9a. We can represent an environmental graph computed by CrowdSim as illustrated in Fig. 3.9b.

- A *birth context* called birth;
- Three *motion contexts* called corridor, corridor2, and corridor3; and
- Three goal contexts: *decision*, *goal1*, and *goal2*.

Associated with this navigation graph is a navigation mesh consisting of the polygons which describe the regions in the environment. Based on these meshes, vertices are calculated (center of each polygon, and the center of each edge which

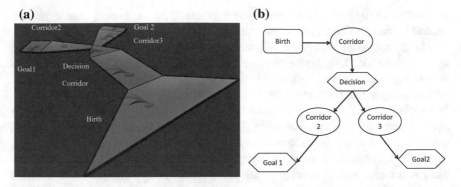

Fig. 3.9 Simple simulation environment comprising different kinds of contexts (**a**) and its respective navigation graph computed by CrowdSim (**b**) (different shapes in the graph mean contexts with different purposes)

represents the doors). This information together with polygons describe the regions and possible paths for all agents.

When the environment is coherently mapped and the user has defined all the *population data*, it is possible to specify in the sub-module *Population Manager* how agents should behave when moving. Agent behaviors can be as follows:

- *Goal Seeking*: The agents should seek their goals directly, or vaguely, by performing random motion;
- *Keep waiting*: The agents, when achieving some specific region of the environment, can spend some time in it before looking for another goal; and
- *Perform random motion*: The agents can chose random destinations during a specific time, before trying to identify the best path to achieve the main goal.

In CrowdSim, we can set up two different categories of behaviors: *static* and *dynamic*:

- *Static behaviors* are always performed as defined by the environment and population manager specifications.
- *Dynamic behaviors* can be configured in the same way as *static behaviors*, but they will be performed only when a trigger is reached. Thus, the responsibility of the *Event Manager* sub-module is to define triggers to perform a series of specific behaviors. An event trigger is composed of the time to occur, a set of dynamic behaviors to be performed at that time, and a time interval between event occurrences. When a dynamic behavior is performed it is possible to set new values to agents attributes, e.g., goals and speed, in order to reproduce the desired behavior.

The correct definition of scenarios is critical in this work, because the combination and analysis of information is responsible for producing acceptable and valid results. When the environment is totally verified with all walkable regions defined, all the parameters configured, and desired behaviors specified, the user is able to run the second module of CrowdSim: Simulation.

The data transfer between configuration and simulation modules is performed by a scenario file (XML), able to store all the configurations to be observed when computing a simulation. In addition to the XML file, the Configuration Module also generates a navigation graph with the initial distributed population in the nodes. We implemented a planner that runs offline from CrowdSim to read the graph and generate evacuation plans. The main difference between a navigation plan and an evacuation plan is that in the former we know where people start and in the latter we define the distribution of people at any graph bifurcation, i.e., we define the exits for each person or group. Of course, we adopt the important hypothesis that the shortest path is not always the best for crowd simulation.

The simulation module of CrowdSim is responsible for computing the navigation of virtual agents in a specific environment. Such navigation should coherently take into account agent motion, collision control, speed variation, and other pedestrian behaviors. A simulation setup, previously defined in the configuration module, is requested as input to the simulation. The simulation computes the routes of each agent to achieve a specific goal, based on the possible paths. Routes can be computed based on user specification (i.e., a graph determined by the user) or computed by a best path algorithm considering only distance criteria. CrowdSim uses A* (Hart et al. 1972) in order to compute shortest paths and collision-free paths, if obstacles are declared. During motion simulation, CrowdSim avoids collisions among agents using a simple local geometry method.

The method for collision avoidance is rule-based and locally defined based on distance proximity. Close agents and their speeds are used in the collision test to detect a possible collision situation in the next frame. If this situation is going to happen, one of the involved agents (randomly defined) must take a decision: (*i*) to change its direction vector (shifts of $\pm 40°$ are allowed) as a function of its goal vector, or (*ii*) to reduce its speed. The information about the pair of agents and the decision taken is saved in a list of past actions, which is lost each second. If a new collision situation is detected for the same pair of agents and there is still an action in the list of past actions, the agent takes a different decision, i.e., if direction-changing is saved in past actions, then a speed change should be performed. Consequently, agents try to reach their goal, avoiding collisions with others. This method is not guaranteed to be collision free, but a maximum error of 10% has been observed in all experiments performed with CrowdSim.

The output of each simulation contains the following information:

- Agent trajectories during the simulation;
- Speed variation for each agent;
- Agent simulation time;
- Total time of simulation, and
- Local density per time step; we compute the local density by counting the number of agents per square meter in each context, rather than the global density (i.e., number of people divided by the building area).

The output data is stored and can be used to produce different statistical analyses. Agent trajectories can be easily exported to be visualized with realistic articulated virtual humans in a graphics engine. Some real-life case studies have applied Crowd-Sim and are discussed in Chap. 4.

3.2.2 Simulation of Heterogeneous Agents

An important aspect in crowd behaviors is how individual factors can influence crowd evolution. For instance: is the crowd dynamics affected if all or some of its members are not in their perfect physical or mental state? A crowd simulation must know when individualism is relevant since heterogeneous crowds (compared to homogeneous crowds) introduce added complexities.

The original CrowdSim implementation only dealt with homogeneous crowds, i.e., where every agent has exactly the same action, namely, to evacuate the environment by following its predefined path as chosen by the shortest path or a defined evacuation plan. In this section, we describe an extension of CrowdSim which includes heterogeneous agents. One specific motivation was to simulate the influence of alcohol, or other drugs, on individual behaviors. One of the few studies undertaken in order to simulate people under the influence of alcohol was by Moore et al. (2008). The authors consider the hypothesis that when under alcoholic influence, people may perform different behaviors including violent and aggressive actions. They implemented a particle model to validate this hypothesis. According to the authors, under alcohol influence people can be aggressive when concentrated in small areas. On the other hand, Moore also reaffirms features that people perform in usual conditions (without alcohol), such as self-organization, walking in lanes, and the principle of least effort.

We have been interested in investigating how differences in individual behaviors can influence the simulated crowd. Inspired by available literature from the World Health Organization, we added to CrowdSim the capability to simulate the behavior of agents affected by alcohol, as in a nightclub, discussed further in Sect. 4.5.1. Table 3.1 lists some effects of alcohol as measured by the Blood Alcohol Concentration (BAC) in the body (World Health Organization 2007). We included just some of the effects described in the original table because many of them could not be considered in our simulations, e.g., "Decrease in various brain center functions."

We implemented an individual attribute in the CrowdSim agents called *goals persistence*, which represents how much the agents seek goals during the simulation. Reducing this attribute value models decreased attention and slowed reaction effects. The method relates the main characteristics of each BAC (World Health Organization 2007) level (each agent k is initialized with a BAC value BAC_k) and the agent goal persistence ($0 <= gp_k <= 1$).

Goals persistence of agent k is defined through:

$$gp_k = \alpha \times e^{(-\beta \times BAC_k)}, \tag{3.1}$$

Table 3.1 Partially used table from WHO (2007)

BAC (g/100ml)	Effects on the body (partially from WHO (2007))
<0.01	Nothing
0.01–0.05	Inconsistent effects on behavioral task performances
0.06–0.10	Decreased attention, slowed reactions, impaired coordination,
0.10–0.15	Dramatic slowing of reactions, impairment of balance and movement
0.16–0.29	Several sensory and motor impairments
0.30–0.39	Nonresponsive stupor, loss of consciousness, death
>0.39	Reduced muscle strength, reduced ability to make rational decisions unconsciousness, death

where $\alpha = 1$, i.e., the value of goal persistence when $BAC_k = 0$. $\beta = 7.44$ and represents a decay constant. We chose an exponential function to represent gp_k; based on the textual description of alcohol effects, degradation is clearly not linear. Based on gp_k, we compute directly how many frames from next f frames that agent k should seek the goal: $nf_k = gp_k \times f$. This means that in next nf_k from f frames, agent k is going to seek the goal, so in the remaining $f - nf_k$ agent k is going to move randomly.

Section 4.5.1 describes this method applied in a case study.

3.2.3 Graphical Visualization of Simulations

We developed a 3D visualization prototype in order to visualize our results using animated virtual humans. Developed with Unity 3D[27] the prototype receives as input a trajectories file, generated as output from a simulation, like the one exemplified in Listing 3.1.

Listing 3.1 XML trajectories file

```
<SIMULATION>
    <FRAMES Quantity = 2>
        <FRAME FrameId = 0>
          <AGENT AgentId = 0>
             <POSITION >4.62   -4.96  0.11 </POSITION>
          </AGENT>
          <AGENT AgentId = 1>
             <POSITION >3.72   -4.96  0.11 </POSITION>
          </AGENT>
          </FRAME>
          <FRAME FrameId = 1>
          <AGENT AgentId = 0>
```

[27]http://unity3d.com.

```
        <POSITION >4.65   −4.96  0.11 </POSITION>
      </AGENT>
      <AGENT AgentId = 1>
        <POSITION >3.75   −4.96  0.11 </POSITION>
      </AGENT>
      </FRAME>
    </FRAMES>
</SIMULATION>
```

The prototype loads all the trajectories and offers the user several options:

1. To select a 3D model to be used as the simulation scenario. This option is non-mandatory; if it is not specified, only trajectories are displayed in the 3D environment.
2. To visualize the trajectories of all the simulation entities, or to verify the trajectory evolution over time.
3. To include 3D virtual humans which will walk according to the trajectories.
4. To verify the heat maps computed based on the trajectory evolution over time. One example of such a heat map is illustrated in Fig. 3.10.

This CrowdSim prototype was used to render all the images illustrated in Sect. 3.3.

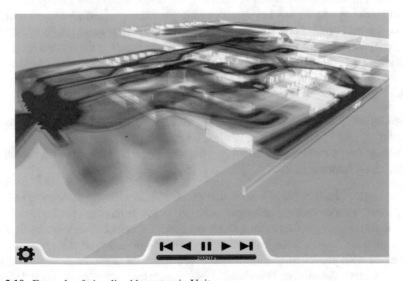

Fig. 3.10 Example of visualized heat map in Unity

3.3   CrowdSim Validation

Given that commercial and research crowd simulation software tools are available, they can provide valuable data on evacuations where real world testing and training can be difficult, uncomfortable, dangerous, and also have ethical implications. When in fire drills, building occupants typically exit at a leisurely pace, without having to deal with panic-inducing events such as smoke-filled corridors, fires in unexpected places, or blocked fire exits (Ren et al. 2006). While it is easy to understand the application of such simulation technologies, it is crucial to understand the importance of validation in this context. To reproduce real-life behavior in evacuation, it is very important to validate the accuracy of the employed simulator.

Based on software engineering principles, *Validation & Verification* are two of the most important software development activities (Adrion et al. 1982; Beizer 1984). These guarantee that software is correctly built and meets its stated requirements. We present how the validation process was performed in CrowdSim. We assume as *validation* the systematic comparison of CrowdSim predictions with reliable information.

The validation of crowd simulators have been addressed through different scientific approaches. The work of Kuligowski and Gwynne [2005] presents a set of guidelines to be observed as general requirements of crowd modeling on simulation software. The authors attempted to aid users in the selection of an appropriate evacuation model by identifying key factors and explanations regarding project requirements, the background of the model, the current capabilities and characteristics of the model for comparison with other models, and the future progress of a model for a specific application. Furthermore, the authors observe that besides knowing the software, it is necessary to have knowledge of crowd behavior. Here, we adopt the following concepts for:

- **Validation**: The computational model is able to provide an acceptable representation of "real life" evacuation situations; and
- **Verification**: It can be established that the theoretical definitions of the model are coherently implemented.

The work of Ronchi (2011) stated that evacuation models are increasing in complexity as the understanding of human behavior in fire progresses, but there is a lack of understanding regarding evacuation model user experiences and needs. In order to ascertain the desires of the evacuation modeling community, an online survey was developed with participants from 36 different countries. Results show that model users consider validation and verification as the most important factor when defining which model to use.

Haron et al. described the evaluation process carried out to determine the most suitable software for studying the evacuation of Al-Masjid An-Nabawi in Haron et al. [2012]. The authors compare the cost–benefit relationship of three off-the-shelf software systems. Galea (1998) presents a set of software validations to be performed.

According to the author there are at least four forms of validation and testing that evacuation models should undergo:

1. *Component Testing* involves checking that the various components of the software perform as desired. This involves running the software through a battery of elementary test scenarios to ensure that the major subcomponents of the model are functioning as intended;
2. *Functional Validation* involves checking that the model possesses the ability to exhibit the range of capabilities required to perform the intended simulations. This requirement is task specific. To satisfy functional verification the model developers must set out in a comprehensible manner the complete range of model capabilities and inherent assumptions and give a guide to the correct use of these capabilities;
3. *Quantitative Validation* involves comparing model predictions with reliable data generated from evacuation demonstrations; and
4. *Qualitative Validation* concerns the nature of predicted human behavior with informed expectations. While this is only a qualitative form of verification, it is nevertheless important, as it demonstrates that the behavioral capabilities built into the model are able to produce realistic behaviors.

The safety engineering field already recognizes these four sets of tests to validate evacuation systems.[28] In London, the International Maritime Organization (IMO) developed *guidelines for evacuation analysis for new and existing passengers ships* IMO (2007) based on Galea's work. The goal is to validate and verify tools able to simulate an evacuation process. Such a guide aims to develop a methodology for conducting an advanced evacuation analysis in order to built systems coherently able to:

- identify and eliminate congestion regions which may arise during an abandonment, due to normal movement of passengers and crew along escape routes, taking into account the possibility that crew may need to move along these routes in a direction opposite to the movement of passengers;
- demonstrate that escape arrangements are sufficiently flexible to provide the possibility that certain escape routes, assembly stations, embarkation stations, or survival craft may be unavailable as a result of a casualty.

We can now detail the set of tests suggested by IMO in order to validate Crowd-Sim, in particular, component testing, qualitative, and quantitative validation. We aim, in the future, to investigate ways to validate CrowdSim according to functional requirements. The next sections explain the performed tests for each category.

---

[28]This procedure has been highlighted in ISO document ISO/TR 13387-8:1999.

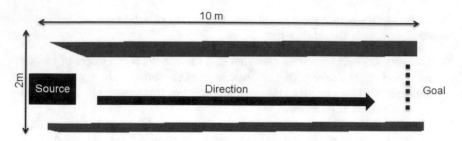

Fig. 3.11 Environment of walking speed test

3.3.1 Component Testing

Component testing is part of the normal development cycle and involves checking if the various components of the software perform as intended. This involves running the software through two elementary test scenarios. In the following, we present a list of adopted component tests extracted from IMO (2007) and applied in CrowdSim.

(A) Maintaining Set Walking Speed on a Corridor:

The first component test defined on the IMO guidelines validates the speed of a single agent when moving in a specific known environment. We built a 2 m wide and and 10 m long corridor (illustrated in Fig. 3.11) and simulated one agent walking from left to right with speed of 1 m/s. The success criteria of this test assumes that the agent should walk 10 m in 10 s.

After ten individual simulations, given an average speed as 1 m/s and standard deviation 0.2, we compute acceptable average values (presented in Table 3.2). The obtained average individual speed was 1.08 m/s with standard deviation of 0.09 m/s. The average walked distance was 10.232 m (standard deviation of 0.097 m) and time of 9.506 s (standard deviation 0.769 s). According to the IMO specifications we observe that CrowdSim successfully achieves this criteria.

(B) Rounding Corners:

This test evaluates the agent's ability to walk around a corner without colliding with walls and other agents. We simulated 20 people approaching a left-hand corner according to specifications illustrated in Fig. 3.12a.

According to the IMO guidelines, this test aims to verify two specific points:

1. *The agents should successfully navigate around the corner without penetrating the boundaries.* Figure 3.12b illustrates the simulated trajectories of all 20 agents. A visual check shows that agents do not collide with the walls.
2. *The agents should successfully navigate without overlap at any time.* Figure 3.13 illustrates three situations for a typical simulation at different moments. While it is difficult to visually verify collision avoidance, we compute the agents' positions file (generated in the simulation) and observe that there are no overlaps among agents (computed by their interpersonal distances).

Table 3.2 Summarized data after 10 random simulations of corridor scenario

Agent ID	Speed (m/s)	Walked distance (m)	Simulated time (s)	AVG vel. (m/s)
1	0.95	10.3	10.8	0.95
2	0.99	10.28	10.16	1.01
3	1	10.05	9.84	1.02
4	1.02	10.32	983	1.04
5	1.04	10.18	9.54	1.06
6	1.07	10.15	9.16	1.10
7	1.1	10.18	9.83	1.03
8	1.11	10.19	8.83	1.15
9	1.13	10.39	8.83	1.17
10	1.2	10.23	8.16	1.25
AVG's	1.06	10.23	9.49	1.08
Standard deviation	0.07	0.09	0.76	0.08

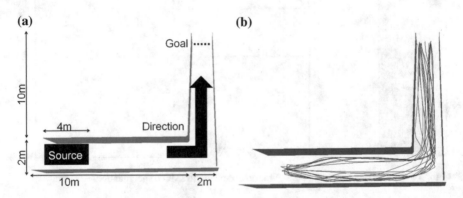

Fig. 3.12 Setup of the experiment environment (**a**) and obtained trajectories of rounding corner simulation (**b**)

3.3.2 Qualitative Validation

Qualitative Validation concerns the nature of predicted human behavior with informed expectations from observed situations. While this is only a qualitative form of verification, it is nevertheless important, as it demonstrates that the capabilities built into the model are able to produce realistic behaviors, i.e., as expected by human beings. The qualitative tests performed in order to validate the CrowdSim simulator are the impact of counter flow in evacuation time, crowd dissipation from a large public room, and exit route allocation. These tests are described next.

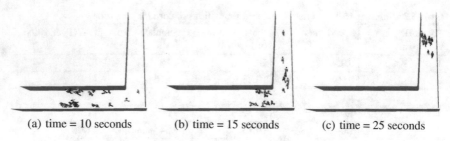

(a) time = 10 seconds   (b) time = 15 seconds   (c) time = 25 seconds

Fig. 3.13 Simulation for rounding corner test, **a** time = 10 s, **b** time = 15 s, **c** time = 25 s

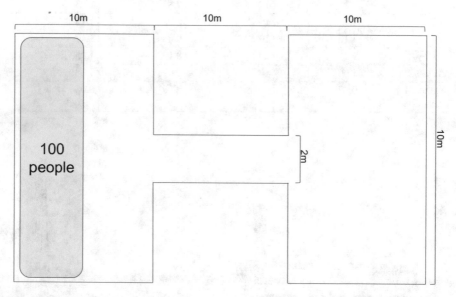

Fig. 3.14 Counterflow scenario configuration according to IMO's specifications

(A) Counter Flow—Impact in Evacuation Time in Two Rooms Connected by a Corridor:

This test was performed according to the environment illustrated in Fig. 3.14 populated by 100 individuals. The test was implemented in two steps described as follows:

1. Agents move from room 1 (left) to room 2 (right), where the initial distribution is such that the space of room 1 is filled from the left with maximum density. The elapsed time until the last person enters room 2 is recorded.
2. Step one was repeated with an additional 10, 50, and 100 people in room 2. People from both rooms move simultaneously to the other room, and the time for the last person in room 1 to enter room 2 is recorded. The expected result is that the recorded time increases as the number of people in the counter flow increases.

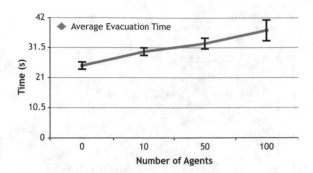

Fig. 3.15 Average and standard deviation of time for evacuation from room 1 as a function of the number of agents in counter flow

We repeated each of the scenarios described in steps 1 and 2 ten times, considering different seeds for the random number generator, which led to a test bank of 40 simulations. The expectation of increasing the time for evacuation of room 1 with the increasing number of agents in counter flow was observed, as shown in Fig. 3.15. The graph in this figure illustrates the average time variation with the number of agents in counter flow. The black markers near to each point represent the standard deviation for the ten simulations in each case.

The conclusion is that CrowdSim performed as expected in this test.

(B) Exit Flow: Crowd Dissipation from a Large Public Room:

This test was performed in a public room populated by 1000 agents, where 4 exits are available during evacuation as illustrated in Fig. 3.16. According to the IMO instructions, the test should run according to two steps: first, simulate and record the time for the last person to leave the room when 4 exits are available and second, the same situation but considering doors 1 and 2 as closed.

The success criteria for this test is related to the amount of time for evacuation in the two cases. According to IMO, the elapsed time of the second case should be around 50% greater than in case 1. When such an experiment was performed with CrowdSim, we computed the time of 83.79 s in the first case and 121.62 s in the second. These values meet the requirement and, as a consequence, we can consider that CrowdSim is validated according to this criteria.

(C) Exit Route Allocation:

The IMO specification for this test requires building a cabin corridor section populated as indicated in Fig. 3.17a. The success criteria for the test assumes that:

1. The main exit was allocated as the goal for the people from cabins 1, 2, 3, 4, 7, 8, 9, and 10.
2. The secondary exit was allocated as the goal for all the remaining passengers.

We performed such a test in CrowdSim where the agents move to their assigned exits. Figure 3.17b presents the agents' trajectories in the 3D environments illustrating the success of the test. It is important to highlight here that we defined shortest path as the parameter to be used by the crowd.

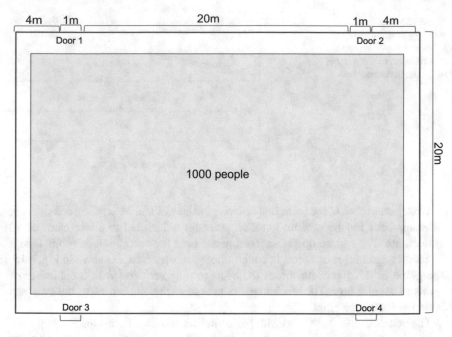

Fig. 3.16 Exit flow scenario configuration according to the IMO specifications

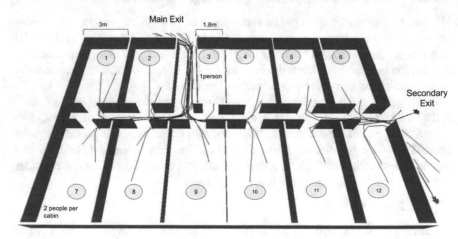

Fig. 3.17 Exit route allocation validation case

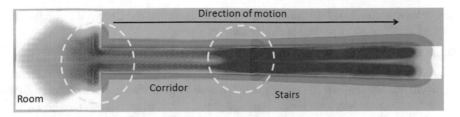

Fig. 3.18 Illustration of stair case validation. It is possible to observe success criteria at the room door as well as in front of the stairs

(D) Staircase:

This test requires building an environment where a room (5 m × 6 m) is connected to a stair by a corridor (2 m × 12 m). Then a population of 150 agents need to be created inside the room and move through the stair. The expected result is that congestion appears at the exit from the room, which produces a steady flow in the corridor with the formation of congestion at the base of the stairs. Figure 3.18 presents a heat map built according to this case simulation. Based on visual inspection, it is possible to observe two bottleneck regions (highlighted in the Figure) which match with the success criteria.

3.3.3 Quantitative Verification

Quantitative verification involves comparing model predictions with reliable data generated from evacuation demonstrations. Galea's work highlights (Galea 1998) two kinds of quantitative validation: *historic* and *prediction* based validation. In the first case, the user knows the results from previous simulations and real exercises. The second case involves using the model to perform predictive simulations prior to having experimental results.

To the best of our knowledge, the current IMO guidelines do not have any validated experimental data in order to allow a thorough quantitative verification of egress models. Therefore, in this work, we propose a method to quantitatively validate CrowdSim.

The quantitative validation should take into account other information besides the total evacuation time. Such information is based on the simulation model outputs and should include, not exclusively, data as exit selection, behavior in different conditions, bottlenecks regions, and exit and finish times. On the other hand, the level and quality of quantitative validation is dependent on the completeness and quality of the reported data (Galea 1998).

Wherever possible, the simulations performed by CrowdSim have been quantitatively evaluated. Several data analysis from simulation data have been undertaken in order to validate simulation results. For the purposes of the CrowdSim validation, we present results of several performed comparisons:

- CrowdSim was used to simulate the evacuation of a night club that was also part of a real egress exercise (Cassol et al. 2015). In this project, we were able to record data from real life in order to contrast with CrowdSim predictions. Such recorded date includes local and global times, local and global densities and speeds (see Sects. 4.5 and 4.3). The analysis of simulated data allowed us to verify some attention points validated during the real egress exercise: *(i)* region of highest density (stairs); *(ii)* we have estimated a greater density of 5.4 people per sqm while in real life, the maximum value was 4.5 people per sqm. *(iii)* the greater density was observed at second 40 of the simulation, while at second 50 during real egress exercise; *(iv)* the observed times of simulation and real life were coherent.
- we also applied CrowdSim to reproduce crowd behavior when evacuating a college building. An analysis of the extracted data from real and simulation scenarios allows us to observe that: *(i)* times observed in simulated and real scenarios, though different, are coherent. We believe that the difference occurs because all the simulation agents were created and started to move at the exact same time, in a different way from real life, where people have different initial response times to events. Also real people do not feel panic voluntarily, since they know that a egress exercise is not a real act of panic; and *(ii)* The analysis of the simulation results allows us to compute the density of the place during the simulated evacuation process and address attention points.

We know that this process for quantitative validation is still simple due to the lack of rich information captured during an egress event (real life or simulation). However, this information was used by the managers of the night club and college building in order to improve their evacuation processes. Detailed information on such projects are presented in the case studies described in Chap. 4.

3.3.4 Observing Emergent Behaviors in CrowdSim

Additionally to CrowdSim validation, according to the IMO scenarios, we are interested in checking the software capability in reproducing self-organization phenomena. We know, as previously explained in Sect. 2.1.1, that crowds can perform some emergent behaviors under specific circumstances.

When performing different simulations, we were able to observe that some self-organization phenomena have emerged in CrowdSim. Figure 3.19 illustrates such behaviors: arch formation (a), also visualized with virtual humans (b), and lane formation (c).

These detected behaviors emerged without any explicitly coded criteria or rule in order to influence such formations.

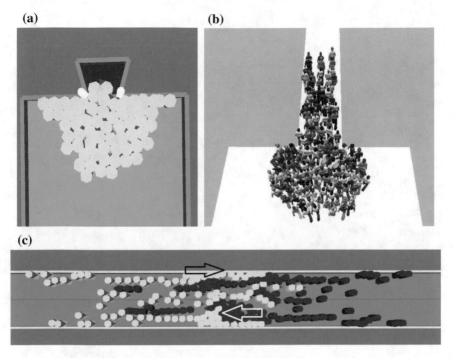

Fig. 3.19 Emergent behaviors observed during CrowdSim validation: Arch formation (**a**), also visualized with virtual humans (**b**) and lane formation (**c**)

3.4 Summary

In this chapter, we have presented some technologies to provide crowd simulation. First, we gave an overview of many commercial software systems available to produce crowd simulation. It is possible to observe different products which have been employed in areas from advertising to movies, and across engineering, architecture, and safety.

The we described the design, features, and applications of CrowdSim, a crowd simulator which is used to explore several specific problems in this book. In addition, we detailed the software validation process. A set of tests were performed according the IMO (2007) guidelines in different categories (Galea 1998). Furthermore, we complemented the tests indicated by IMO by defining a process that allowed validating CrowdSim in a quantitative way, according to results comparable to real-life scenarios. This can be considered an alternative to the IMO approach to software validation.

Chapter 4
Case Studies

When analyzing an egress process simulation, it is possible to extract data that can be used to provide a deep analysis of scenarios. Before something goes wrong, a simulation project can identify attention points related to people's comfort and safety when in egress.

The data obtained by crowd simulation can be very useful to safety analysis in order to estimate environment conditions and attention points (i.e. bottlenecks regions) as well as to map and understand people behavior during an evacuation process. Although the final evacuation time is commonly the only variable used in the analysis, other information are also important. According to Galea (1998), in addition to total time of evacuation, important information can be considered:

- Bottleneck regions;
- exit selection, exit flow rates, exit start, and end times; and
- agents behaviors in different conditions (e.g., when under smoke and alcohol influence).

With the *thinking of safety* in mind we have applied CrowdSim in a set of case studies performed with the main goal to demonstrate its potentiality in real-world application. Each project contains a different setup, but all of them are concerned with evacuation behaviors.

Each project has allowed us to analyze different populations and also different ways to people leave the specific building. In addition, in each project we ran different simulations setups, aiming to analyze different situations. Moreover, when comparing the obtained results from different simulations in the same environment, we can evaluate the efficacy of alternative evacuation strategies and also the building structure.

This chapter presents, first of all, the common *project pipeline*, applied to all performed case studies. Following, we present a set of performed case studies in different fields.

© Springer International Publishing AG 2017
V.J. Cassol et al., *Simulating Crowds in Egress Scenarios*,
https://doi.org/10.1007/978-3-319-65202-3_4

4.1   Case Studies Pipeline

Despite that each case study considers different buildings and population details, all of the projects followed the same execution pipeline. Such pipeline is illustrated in Fig. 4.1.

During the projects development, for all case studies, we followed 4 commons steps:

1. *Environment Understanding*: A near contact with the building manager is very important in order to understand all the building structure and also its functionality. In addition, building managers also provide some valuable information about how people use to behave in such place. At this point, we try to map and understand the use of doors, corridors and more common routes which are used by people when leaving the environment;

2. *3D Environment Definition*: It is necessary to reproduce the building into a 3D environment. This activity is usually performed by a graphical designer, who reproduces all the building details (doors, corridors, and other obstacles) in a coherent way to real world;

3. *Setup and Simulations*: We define, in the 3D environment, semantic information regarding to represent all the different regions of the place. In CrowdSim, we specify the contexts which details information about the areas where people will be inserted and removed in the simulation. In addition we also map the regions where the motion of pedestrian is allowed (corridors) and population details (number of agents, their goals, etc.). After, we run the simulation in order to compute data to be analyzed; and

4. *Data Analysis*: After the simulations are complete, we analyze the obtained statistical data in a different way. The goal is to map aspects of people comfort and safety when in egress, as well as, to map bottleneck regions and other possible attention points. In order to do this, we inspect the simulation outputs in order to analyze aspects of density of agents, speeds, people distribution along the time, etc. Such information is usually part of a report which is shared with all the project stakeholders.

Follow, we detail each one of the performed case studies were CrowdSim was applied.

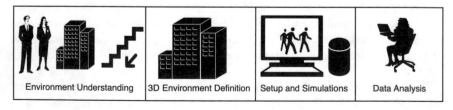

Fig. 4.1 Common pipeline of performed case studies

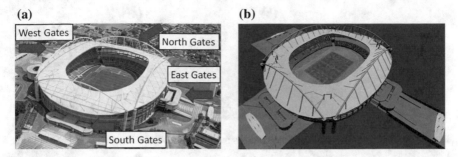

Fig. 4.2 In **a** is presented a real view of the Olympic Stadium where is highlighted the four areas of access to audience; while in **b** we illustrate a 3D representation of the stadium

4.2 Evacuation of Olympic Stadium

In this case study, we have applied CrowdSim in order to study the evacuation process of a football stadium. The Brazilian *Olympic Stadium JÃčo Havelange*, called *Stadium Nilton Santos* since 2010, was built for the *2007 Pan American Games* and according to the stadium managers can be considered as the most modern stadium of Latin America and number five in the world.[1] The stadium, site of Brazilian soccer team Botafogo,[2] has capacity of 46,000 people. The project was performed as a partnership between authors insitution (PUCRS) and Botafogo soccer team with the main goal to provide a study of the crowd egress process in the stadium. The factors considered in the analyzes represent information of people comfort (density of people) and also the total time of evacuation.

A representation of the stadium is illustrated in Fig. 4.2. The stadium can be accessed by four distinct areas, as presented in Fig. 4.2a. The detailed understanding of the stadium structure, i.e. gates and corridors, is very important when staring a crowd simulation project. This is because the first phase in the project is concerned with the modeling of the 3D environment (a 3D representation of the stadium is illustrated in Fig. 4.2b).

When building the 3D model of the stadium is important to take into account all the physical constraints existing in the real stadium. The doors size, corridors dimensions and the existence of obstacles should exist in 3D model. Figure 4.3 presents common areas of the stadium that were considered when developing the 3D model.

Another important aspect considered in this project was the correct specification of the grandstand areas. In Fig. 4.4, it is possible to observe such areas (red floor and green chairs) and the regions defined to allow the motion of pedestrians (blue). Considering such definition, when an event occurs, e.g., the end of a match, the individuals are able to leave their seats and find the best way to leave the stadium.

---

[1] http://bfr.com.br/estadioniltonsantos.php.

[2] http://bfr.com.br.

(a)   **(b)**   **(c)**

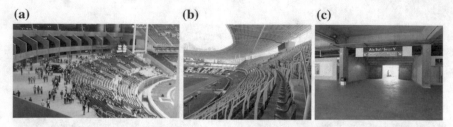

Fig. 4.3 Three representations of common areas in the stadium, including grandstand and corridor regions, where people are allowed to walk

Fig. 4.4 Example of simulation configuration considering grandstand areas

In this project, we simulated three different situations considering information about historic of matches provided from the stadium managers:

1. The average of population during some observed matches: approximately 17,000 people;
2. full capacity: approximately 46,000 people; and
3. a test case where we considered the full capacity of the stadium together with the unavailability of one exit (see Fig. 4.5).

It is important to highlight that all agents agents know their best exit, even when one exit was closed, the agents knew that and went directly to the second best exit. After the simulations, we performed some statistical analyzes that have allowed us to highlight some points:

- In all simulated situations the agents were able to walk in a speed close to their desired speed (average speed = 1.2 m/s);
- We did not observe regions with higher densities ($\geq$ 4people/sqm) in any scenario;
- The average time of all scenarios was around 7 min.

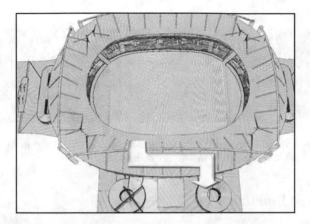

Fig. 4.5 Illustration of 1 unavailable exit in the stadium

(a) Simulating zooming two of the exits.   (b) Crowd evacuating the Olympic Stadium.

Fig. 4.6 Visual representation of egress performance in the stadium

Based on such analysis, we could say that the "well-behaved" evacuation in the football stadium should occur in safe time. Of course, this time can be bigger if people do not decide to leave the stadium in the same time (as commonly occurs during an end-match situation) or if some other situation occurs, e.g., explosion (can affect the environment) or panic (can affect people behavior). Figure 4.6 illustrates two moments of the simulations in the stadium.

The 3D environment of the stadium is available at extra directory from Springer.[3] In addition, a video case of the project is currently available.[4]

---

[3] http://extras.springer.com/.
[4] https://youtu.be/RRNu10ubUHw.

(a)   (b)   (c)

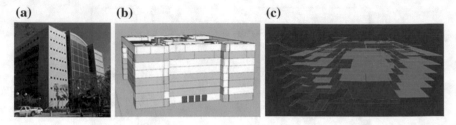

Fig. 4.7 Three representations of the building simulated in this case study: the real building (**a**), 3D environment (**b**), and simulation environment defined in *CrowdSim*.

4.3 College Building

In this case study, we applied CrowdSim in order to reproduce pedestrian behaviors when leaving the Faculty of Informatics (FACIN) building at PUCRS.[5] The building is composed by eight floors, where it is possible to identify class rooms (floors 2, 3, 4, and 5), professors offices, research labs (floors 6 and 7) and business offices (floors 1, 7, and 8). Furthermore, there are two emergency exits that are accessed by stairs from all floors. The population of the building is around 800 people every day. This scenario is illustrated in Fig. 4.7 where we can observe a real external picture of the building (a), as well as the respective 3D model (b), and the building environment represented in CrowdSim (c).

The 3D virtual environment was modeled by a 3D designer using Sketch Up[6] according to the building's floorplans. Each floor of the building is coherent with the real environment dimensions. The illustration of the first floor is presented in Fig. 4.8 where the two emergency exits previously described (one in the front and other in the back of the building) are highlighted. For this case study, the furniture inside the building is not considered in the simulation.

For the simulation, the full environment is mapped in order to specify walkable regions for the agents. This process is performed by CrowdSim configuration module (see Fig. 4.7c). The green areas represent the *starting* areas, regions where the agents can be created, while the external areas of the building (*goal* areas) are presented in red and are located near to emergency exits. Connecting *start* and *goal* areas, we can observe the *walkable* areas (corridors and stairs) illustrated in blue.

To set up the simulation scenario, we take into account the average number of people at each floor of the building, during a normal day. Table 4.1 summarizes the numbers of simulated people. It is important to mention that this population distribution was similar when performing the real evacuation exercise.

The high concentration of people in the first four floors is mainly because in this area are located most part of the classrooms and practical laboratories for classes. In the other floors are located research labs, professors, and business offices. In the

---

[5]www.pucrs.br/facin.

[6]http://www.sketchup.com/.

Fig. 4.8 Illustration of the building first floor

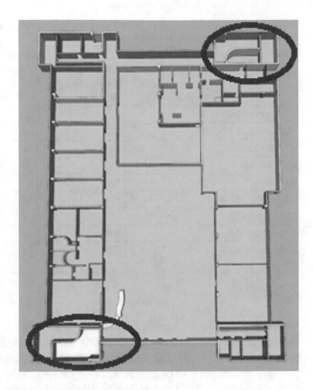

Table 4.1 Population simulated in each floor of the college building

Floor	1	2	3	4	5	6	7	8	Total
Agents	100	190	200	130	85	55	50	20	830

performed simulation, all the agents are configured to leave the building using emergency exits except the agents from first floor. The same orientation was considered when performed the real evacuation exercise.

Table 4.2 summarizes the obtained information from real and simulated evacuation process. The evacuation times are presented in seconds. In order to measure time, two aspects were defined:

1. *Safe Areas*: We consider as a safe area the building region located after the emergency exit on each floor. More specifically, these areas represent the stairs used during the evacuation.
2. *Outside Areas*: The goal areas outside the building.

In the real egress exercise, we had the collaboration of some volunteers who timed their walk time until they reach the safe and goal areas. Unfortunately, in some rooms, we could not have information. A quick analyzes of the extracted data from real and simulation scenarios allows us to observe that the differences are small and coherent.

Table 4.2 Summarized data from college building evacuation: real and simulated process. Some cells are empty because we could not obtain the data in real life

Place	Real Process		Simulation	
	Time to first person achieve the safe area	Time to first person leave the building	Time to first agent achieve the safe area	Time to first agent leave the building
Classroom 205	30		32	56
Classroom 214	35	100	34	64
Classroom 301		180	52	68
Lab 309	40	163	38	76
Lab 310	25	120	16	64
Classroom 312		154	57	116
Classroom 412		312	54	132
Classroom 415		300	41	118
Professors room (5th floor)		274	55	159

We believe that the difference between the simulation and the real exercise time is because all the simulation agents were created and started to move in the exact same time, in a different way from real life, where people have different response time to events. Another point to be considered is regarding to the agents velocity. According to literature Fruin (1971b), we specify the velocity of the agents in 0.8 m/s adding a positive and negative variation of 20%.

Analyzing just the classroom 309, we can observe a divergence between the simulation time (76 s) and real process time (163 s). After contacting people from classroom 309, we were informed that they decide to organize their bags and scholar material before leaving. We consider that is a reaction that should not happen in a real emergency event and it contributed for the large difference between the reported times.

After the simulation finished, we observed that the time taken for all the agents leave the building was 250 s (4 min and 10 s). On the other hand, the last person to leave the building in the real evacuation exercise left at time of 7 min and 34 s (454 s). Again, it is important to do not only focus on the time difference, since people in real life do not put their self in emergence situation voluntarily.

The analyzes of the simulation results provided by CrowdSim allows us to compute the density of the place during the simulated evacuation process. The density analysis makes possible to identify attention points in the environment including bottlenecks. In Fig. 4.9 we present a density map where we illustrate the environment density, specifically on the stairs located on the frontal emergency exit in two distinct moments of simulation (after 40 (a) and 80 (b) seconds of simulation). The regions in red mean attention areas (more than 2 people per sqm) while the yellow and green areas mean regions with medium (2 people per sqm) and low (1 person

(a)   **(b)**

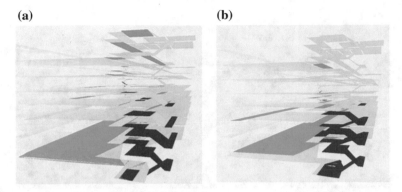

Fig. 4.9 Density maps of college building in two distinct moments of simulation (after 40 (**a**) and 80 (**b**) seconds of simulation

per sqm) concentration of people. Unfortunately, we do not have such measures in real drill, but people testimonials mention that emergency stairs was crowded from the 4th floor.

As observed in real drill, the greater concentration points, in the simulation, were located between the first and the fourth floors. The high concentration in these regions starts after 40 s of simulation when agents from highest floors achieve half of distance to reach the goal areas outside the building. As in last experiment, the 3D environment of the stadium is available at extra directory from Springer.[7]

4.4 School

In this case study we applied CrowdSim in a school that receive kindergartens, elementary, middle and high school students. The project was performed at Pastor Dohms School,[8] in Porto Alegre—Brazil. The first step was to reproduce the school in a 3D environment as requested input. Subsequently, we defined the environment constraints as well as the desired behaviors according to the steps enumerated as follows:

1. We specified the regions where motion is allowed (e.g., corridors and stairs) in the 3D environment. Moreover we defined the regions where the agents should be created (i.e., class rooms) and the regions to be considered as goals (i.e., exit doors). Such information is taken into account by CrowdSim when running path planing in order to compute agents routes. Figure 4.10 illustrates the school 3D model (a) and the environment mapped into CrowdSim in (b).

---

[7]http://extras.springer.com/.

[8]http://dohms.org.br/.

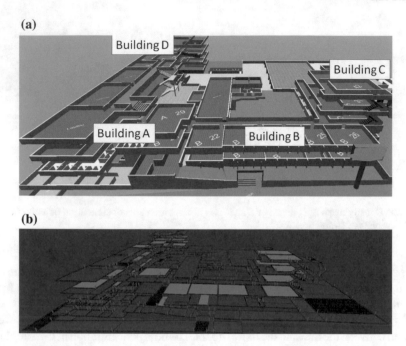

Fig. 4.10 The school environment modeled in 3D (**a**) and the environment specification in Crowd-Sim (**b**)

2. The population data was defined according to school staff specifications. We were able to define the number of agents to be simulated as well as their goals during simulation. In order to specify such information, we have considered the values according to the real occupation of the school for each classroom, at each building (as illustrated in Fig. 4.10a). Also, we observed the best school exit to be considered in an egress process according to the school structure. The school has two exits that are considered by the students when leaving the building in normal days. In addition, we observed the existence of extra doors (not used by the students) that are able to be considered by additional routes when thinking about egress process. The school structure allows us to validate different routes for possible egress situation that are further described.

After the environment and population constraints specifications, we performed simulations according to four different scenarios. Such scenarios were defined considering the school population in the morning (1067 students) and afternoon (729 people) as well as available exits (Fig. 4.11 illustrates the available exits considered in the experiments). The four simulated scenarios are as follows:

1. morning population with only the main exits available;
2. afternoon population with only the main exits available;
3. morning population with all exits available;
4. afternoon population with all exits available.

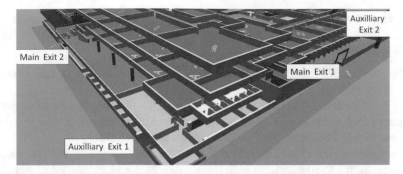

Fig. 4.11 Available exits from the school

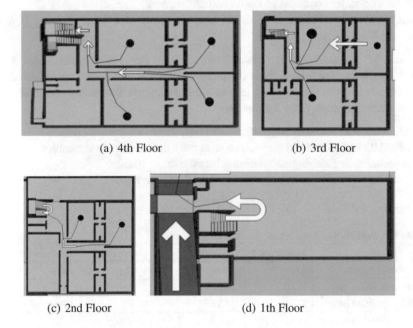

(a) 4th Floor   (b) 3rd Floor

(c) 2nd Floor   (d) 1th Floor

Fig. 4.12 Routes representing the evacuation plan of Building D

In order to test the four scenarios, it was necessary to define routes able to guide the agents until the nearest exit, according to the classrooms' locations. The routes represent, at this point, an evacuation plan to be performed. In this work, four evacuation plans have been developed according to the specification of each evacuation scenario. Figure 4.12 illustrates the routes to be followed by the agents that should leave the Building D of the school. The lines indicate the path to be followed while the white arrows represent the direction of the motion. As previously illustrated in Fig. 4.10a the school is composed by four buildings of classrooms.

Besides setting the evacuation plans (environment and people data, behaviors and routes), it is important to emphasize some points to be observed during the simulation of all scenarios:

- The people distribution per classroom was computed according to data provided from school staff;
- We consider a reaction time for all scenarios. This time represents the response time of each agent until it starts to move after received an orientation to egress. We considered the response time as 5s for all the experiments;
- The agents are not created in the exact same time. In the experiments, we created groups from 1 to 10 agents (in each classroom) observing an interval of 10 s. This procedure was adopted to simulate time of walking into the classroom, since we did not consider obstacles as chairs and tables; and
- All agents aim to move at a certain average speed of 0.8 m/s, having 20% of standard deviation.

Table 4.3 summarizes the obtained results from performed simulations. Also, Fig. 4.13 shows two frames from distinct simulations, which aim to illustrate the two main exits from school taken into account during the simulation of egress. Furthermore, we redefine the 4 simulations:

1. Simulation 1: morning population with only the main exits available;
2. Simulation 2: afternoon population with only the main exits available;
3. Simulation 3: morning population with all exits available;
4. Simulation 4: afternoon population with all exits available.

Table 4.3 Summary of 4 performed simulations

	Simulation 1	Simulation 2	Simulation 3	Simulation 4
Number of agents	1067	729	1067	729
Total evacuation time	217 s	207 s	214 s	172 s
AVG evacuation time	98 s	88 s	88 s	78 s
Smallest evacuation time	31 s	33 s	16 s	16 s
Greater walked distance	132 m	112 m	130 m	103 m
AVG walked distance	74 m	68 m	67 m	59 m
Smaller walked distance	30 m	23 m	21 m	20 m
Higher speed	1.05 m/s	1.059 m/s	1.05 m/s	1.05 m/s
AVG speed	0.81 m/s	0.82 m/s	0.82 m/s	0.81 m/s
Smallest speed	0.29 m/s	0.10 m/s	0.45 m/s	0.13 m/s
Higher observed density	6 people/sqm (sec 61)	4 people/sqm (sec 50)	5 people/sqm (sec 61)	4 people/sqm (sec 60)
AVG of higher densities	2.2 people/sqm	2.2 people/sqm	1.79 people/sqm	1.49 people/sqm
Std dev higher densities	1.87	1.88	1.72	1.34

(a)

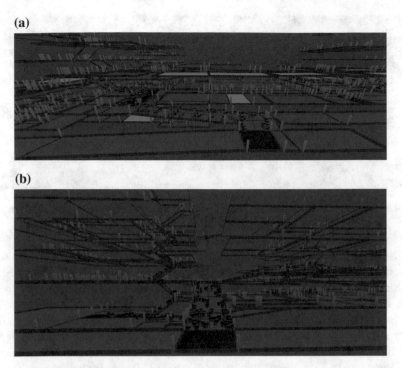

(b)

Fig. 4.13 Two simulation frames illustrating the position of the two main exits of the school

The analyzes of crowd simulation results have allowed us to observe different points of attention during the egress process. One important point is concerned to the variation of density in the buildings of school during the evacuation. The resulting data has shown the time of simulation when the higher density was detected. The estimation of the time for higher density allowed us to analyze the simulation and environment in order to identify the place of high density as an attention region. In the four simulated scenarios, the higher density have occurred in the stair of buildings C (scenarios 1 and 3) and D (scenarios 2 and 4). Figure 4.14 presents two frames of simulation when the highest density was detected on Building C (left) and Building D (right).

At this point, all simulated agents follow the same behavior during the egress. However, one of the concerns from the school manager was related to one special building of the school: Building D, where the kindergarten classrooms are located. We suppose that small kids usually present different behavior of teenagers or adults, specially when they are part of an evacuation process. In order to deal with this situation, we implemented a new rule in CrowdSim: we propose to implement an individual attribute in the agents called "goals persistence", which is related to a factor that represents how much time the agents seek goals during the simulation (it was also used in Sect. 3.2.2).

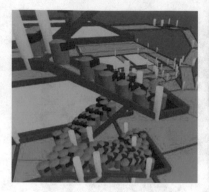

Fig. 4.14 Highest density detected by simulations in Building C (left) and Building D (right)

This factor makes the agents ignore the goal seeking behavior and remain wandering during some specific time. We did not found any specific literature about children behavior in evacuation scenarios, in order to validate our approach. In this way, we empirically applied the factor in order to represent the following case: The children of Building D should perform goal seeking behavior during 2/3 of time than other student. Experimental simulations have shown that the Building D is evacuated in 260 s, when goals persistence factor = 1, i.e. always seeking goal, while the time increases to 325 s when such factor is applied. These simulations could more explored in future researches.

After these simulations, we could observe that CrowdSim is capable to simulate different environments and population characteristics. Finally, we observed that the software is easily adaptable, since we could simulate a population of kindergarten children with just minor modifications in the model. However, we noticed that knowing the numerical output of the software, besides its utility for evaluation of the school safety, does not have education impact for training the children and teenagers in the school. We hardly imagine kids reading a report to learn and understand how to behave in a egress situation. In order to solve that, we developed a game like interactive tool that allows students to embody the simulation results in a more attractive and engaging way. The next section details this improvement.

The Game

One reason for the growing interest in games is the engagement they arouse in the players. In an opposite trend than entertainment, games can also be used to direct this engagement for improving users' learning and training. In that sense, serious games can be thought as an efficient tool to educate and train people aiming to develop, for example, an intrinsic thinking of safety. One point addressed in this project focuses on the importance to engage kids in the training of evacuation processes. Usually, buildings may have hundreds or thousands of occupants and, sometimes, many of them are not aware of the architect layout in order to know the safest exit from their location Gwynne et al. (1999).

When we are working with crowd simulation in safety applications, it is very common to analyze the produced data according some statistical criteria. Once this project was performed at a scholar environment, however, the customer is not only the school managers team. We are very interested in developing a culture of safety on the students and their families. We believe that games can be a powerful tool in order to achieve this goal. Indeed, the use of games to illustrate simulation data have been previously used in approaches from different authors. The *Emergency Evacuation Simulator*[9] used a game engine to develop a tool for training during emergency. In the same way, Schatz et al. (2014) proposes a Building Information Modeling- based serious game able to produce fire safety evacuation simulations.

Aiming to engage the students and make they able to think about safety, we created a game-based interactive visualization tool. The student can learn and really understand as well as virtually be part of a possible egress process from their own school. This tool was called *Game4Safety* and was developed according to the following requirements:

1. *To recreate the realistic training environment (precise 3D model of the school)*: we reproduce the interior of the school according to its physical structure. At first, we do not consider furniture due to the time consuming work necessary to reproduce the details on each classroom. It is important to mention that the approach presented here is able to consider furniture as obstacles if their 3D models was available;
2. *the student should be able to explore the school space in its normal state*: as in First-person-shooter (FPS) game, the player is able to navigate in the environment as one of the characters present on it. Also, the player is also able to navigate as in a Real-Time Strategy (RTS) game;
3. *it must be possible to the users to observe the way out and the shortest routes to the exits from different locations in the environment*: the player must be able to choose a specific classroom in the school. With this feature, the camera is positioned on such point of the environment and the user is able to observe the best route to leave the school from that point. Also, the player can adopt a FPS camera view and move around the environment according the presented route;
4. *to allow time monitoring*: we allow the player to select one specific virtual human to monitor his/her behavior when evacuating; and
5. *to emulate different population scenarios*: when running the game, the player is able to choose among different scenarios to explore. Such set of scenarios represent 4 different simulations performed according to populations on the school during different periods of the day (morning and afternoon) and also the variation of available exits. We considered the normal exits used by students in normal days and also presented scenarios taking into account emergency exits simulating a possible emergency egress process.

---

[9]http://www.program-ace.com/portfolio/case-studies/emergency-evacuation-simulator.

(a)

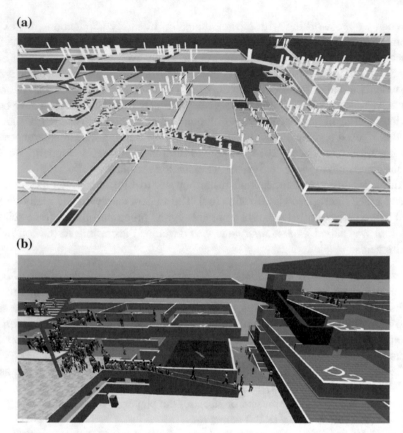

(b)

Fig. 4.15 Illustration of the simulation environment in CrowdSim (**a**), and the same point of view in the game engine (**b**)

In order to meet such features and requirements, a prototype based on Unity 3D game engine[10] was developed. Figure 4.15 illustrates a comparative of a simple simulation visualization in CrowdSim and the same point of view visualized in *Game4Safety*.

By starting *Game4Safety*, the player is able to select one of four available scenarios to be loaded. When the scenario is loaded, the user can interact with the environment and play a simulation. These options are available to the player in the developed interface:

- To choose the best camera to explore the environment (RTS or FPS). Controls are available on keyboard;
- to see the available routes for the virtual humans. The user can also select one specific virtual human by click on it. When a virtual human is selected, specific

---

[10]https://unity3d.com.

Fig. 4.16 Application Controller Interface (a) where it is possible to detail an specific agent (b)

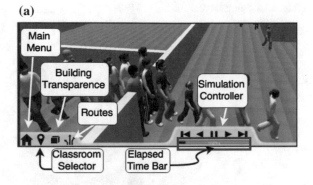

(a)

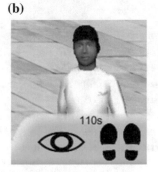

(b)

information about he/she is displayed (e.g., total time to the virtual human leave the school and the followed route)—See Fig. 4.16b. The player can follow the virtual human during the motion or also assume the character point of view;

- To apply transparency in the building in order to better visualize the 3D characters as well as the routes;
- To select a specific classroom and be transported to such location in the virtual environment;
- To increase the speed of visualization, back to initial point and also go to end point of simulation; and
- To visualize the elapsed time of simulation, in seconds.

An illustration of the interface controllers is available in Fig. 4.16a.

In order to verify the efficiency of *Game4Safety*, a supervised play test section was performed. A group composed of 10 students aged from 12 to 15 years and also 2 members of school staff have been part of the validation process of the game. During the play test section the testers were observed by the development team of *Game4Safety* (Fig. 4.17).

After exploring *Game4Safety*, some testimonials from the group of testers have been collected. The overall impression of the group tester was positive and, according to them, very helpful in order to learn how a possible evacuation process can be performed in the school. Some of them are presented next:

Fig. 4.17 Students playing
Game4Safety

- *This is an important tool in order to develop a useful evacuation plan. It is a different approach to develop safety thinking in the students.* (School's Principal).
- *The game is very cool and we can learn when playing. I went to my classroom and now I know how to leave the school when in emergency. It is very important to our safety.* (Student, 13 years).
- *This game can help me and my colleagues to understand and think what is the safest way to leave the school in a possible emergency situation. The game also can help other schools.* (Student, 14 years).

The analyzes of testimonials indicates the positive application of *Game4Safety*. The game is currently used in the school in order to train the students, and also their families about the importance of evacuation scenarios and a culture of safety. The 3D environment of the school is available at extra directory from Springer.[11] In addition, a video case of the project is currently available.[12]

4.5   Night Club

In this section, we detail the application of CrowdSim in a night club, in Porto Alegre, Brazil. Our goal was to study how people perform an evacuation process in real life and thus obtain data to allow quantitative comparisons with our simulator. The experiment was a shared experience developed in partnership with the night club owners and a safety company. On the day the experiment was conducted, the audience agreed to leave the club exactly at 2AM. Some days before the egress exercise in the club, CrowdSim was applied in order to provide different evacuation plans that could be used to estimate occupant behavior. The first step of the process was to reproduce the club environment in 3D. The environment has a total area of

---

[11] http://extras.springer.com/.

[12] https://youtu.be/cVgNuaL6Dw8.

(a)

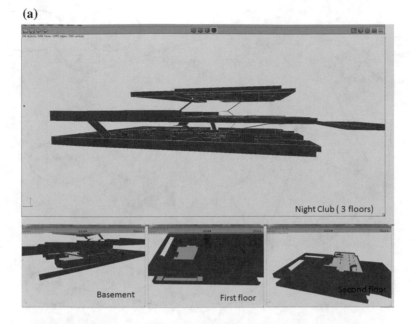

(b)

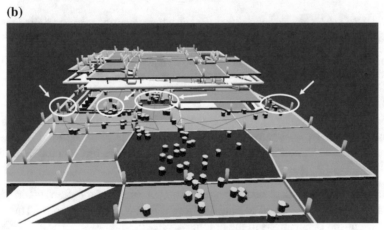

Fig. 4.18 Illustration of the 3D model of the night club into CrowdSim and the location of its exit doors in *CrowdSim*.

1010 sqm and has 4 floors and 4 doors (see Fig. 4.18b to see the door locations). A 3D representation is illustrated in Fig. 4.18a.

The 3D environment was necessary in order to allow the definition of the possible evacuation plans. This is because we specify in the 3D model, all the regions where agents need to be inserted and removed from the simulation and also we specify the regions where the motion is allowed. The specification of the environment, defined in

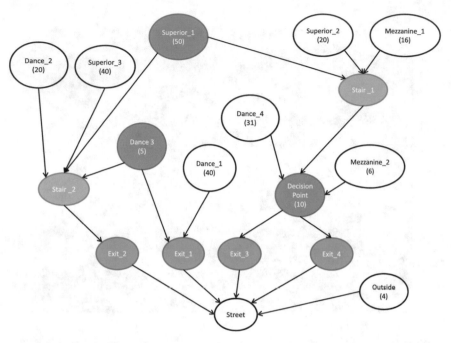

Fig. 4.19 Night club's graph specifying the environment structure to be considered in the generation of possible evacuation routes. All the nodes means walkable regions while the edges represent the doors connecting the rooms of the place. In addition, orange nodes means decision areas (where the agents can chose different paths) while green nodes represent the stairs connecting the different floors of the night club. The graph also presents the population created in each node

the configuration module of CrowdSim according to the 3D model of the club, makes possible to build an environmental graph. Such graph is illustrated in Fig. 4.19 and it is composed by three different types of nodes which are represented by different colors:

1. Orange nodes represent decision areas. In such areas of the club, where agents can be created, they need to chose different routes from that point. This nodes represent the bifurcations in the graph;
2. Green nodes are representing the stairs responsible for connecting the different floors of the club. No agents are created in such regions that are considered just motion areas; and
3. White nodes are regions where agents can be created in the simulation and also, walkable areas. The only exception is the node called *Street* that is responsible for removing the agents in the simulation (exit context).

The safety company had generated different evacuation plans using CrowdSim. In Table 4.4 are the results obtained from three evacuation plans designed and tested in CrowdSim by the safety engineers (see Fig. 4.21 containing two frames from one of the performed simulations). The difference among the 3 evacuated plans (highlighted

Table 4.4 Quantitative data comparing simulated scenarios containing 240 people

	Simulation 1	Simulation 2	Simulation 3
Total time of evacuation (sec)	142	142	146
Average time (sec)	61	62	64
Average density (people/m^2)	0.1123	0.1138	0.1162
Average speed (m/s)	0.80	0.80	0.80
Highest Density	5.4	5.4	5.0
Place of highest density	Stairs (2nd floor)	Stairs (2nd floor)	Stairs (2nd floor)
Time when highest density was observed	Second 40	Second 39	Second 50
Highest speed (m/s)	1.3	1.2	1.3
Smallest speed (m/s)	0.1	0.1	0.05
Number of people in Door1	54	18	21
Number of people in Door2	12	41	50
Number of people in Door3	80	126	75
Number of people in Door4	100	61	100

in Fig. 4.20) is related to the number of people in the 3 bifurcations. Based on such distributions, the number of people who used the exit doors changed, as shown in the last four lines in Table 4.4. Indeed, it is easy to show that doors 3 and 4 received more people than the other two. This happened because doors 3 and 4 are larger and could accommodate more people.

After performing several simulations, it was possible to identify a set of plausible evacuations plans to be performed in the real life exercise. In Table 4.4 we present the results computed of three evacuation plans that have been designed and tested in CrowdSim by the safety engineers.

Plan of Simulation 1 has been selected and used in a real life scenario. Please, note that according to all individual metrics (gt, at, ad, and av) this plan achieved the best or equally the best results. Figure 4.22 specifies the percentage values to indicate the specifications of the chosen plan: how many agents should follow each route available on decision areas of the club (see orange nodes in Fig. 4.19).

Once the plan was selected, the safety company began to train individuals who work in the Night Club. The real evacuation was performed with 240 people who agreed to participate in the experience. During the real egress exercise, we were able to collect different data in order to evaluate results of this experience. Occupant data was obtained from security camera videos. The number of people in different parts of the club was obtained from infrared technology. This information was very important in order to evaluate this work. Table 4.5 summarizes the comparison between real and virtual evacuation scenarios.

Figure 4.23 provides an image captured during the evacuation that shows the people in stairs (2nd floor) at 40 s after the simulation started, and another image at the same place and time in the virtual simulation.

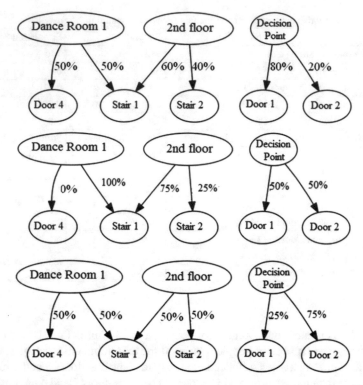

Fig. 4.20 Three examples of evacuation plan tested by our model: Simulations ids: 1, 2 and 3, as related in Table 4.4

Fig. 4.21 Images illustrating the simulation

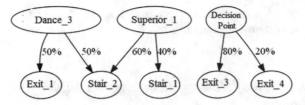

Fig. 4.22 Subgraph illustrating the percentage of agents who should follow by each path of the bifurcations in the graph. This sub-graph represent the reference plan used in real life

Table 4.5 Quantitative data comparing real and simulated worlds considering exactly the same evacuation plan

	Simulation 1	Real-world data
Total time of evacuation (sec)	142	175
Highest density (people/m^2)	5.4	4.5
Place of highest density	Stairs (2nd floor)	Stairs (2nd floor)
Time when highest density was observed	Second 40	Second 50
Highest speed (m/s)	1.3	1.5
Smallest speed (m/s)	0.1	0.2

Fig. 4.23 Images illustrating the stairs in the 2nd floor 40 s after the beginning of the simulation in real and virtual environment

When analyzing Table 4.5, it is clear the difference in total evacuation time. It can be explained by the fact that real people do not voluntarily behave the same as they would in a true emergency. That is, real people, not in panic, respect the space of others, and therefore do not achieve the higher densities presented in the simulation data. As for the others case studies, we make available the 3D environment of the night club at extra information directory from Springer.[13] In addition, a video case of the project is currently available.[14]

4.5.1   Simulation of Heterogeneous Agents Under Alcohol Influence

The emergent characteristics of crowds can represent several independent behaviors; in this way, recent scientific studies have considered crowds as an *entity able to think* McPhail (1991). Such thinking came to endorse the idea that crowds are composed by independent individuals, each one with the own needs and ways of thinking.

The individuality can be represented by many factors as the gender, age of each individual or her/his physical state. An important aspect in crowd behaviors is how such factors can influence on crowd evolution/simulation. The main question of this experiment is: *Can the crowd be affected when its members or part of them are not in their perfect physical or mental state?*

Situations where individual's physical state varies can be observed in mostly all contexts of real life. The important question in the context of crowd simulation is to know when such differences are relevant to be considered in a simulation, since the simulation of heterogeneous crowds (if compared to homogeneous crowds) obviously includes complexities to be dealt with. In this section, we investigate how some differences in individual behaviors (e.g., caused by alcohol) can influence the crowd behavior. Inspired on available literature (World Health Organization[15]) we simulate the behavior of agents affected by alcohol in a nightclub.

We used the night-club simulation (see Sect. 4.5) in order to have simulations that were compared with real life, and presented data could possible be coherent. The difference is that for this time we simulate crowds considering heterogeneous agents in order to represent people under alcohol influence. For this experiment, we worked with a population of 240 people (the same population on the real-life egress exercise presented in Sect. 4.5).

We considered three different scenarios having varied number from total population been affected by BAC level (i.e., simulating percentage of people who drank and how much), please refer to Sect. 3.2.2 for details. The tested BAC levels were: 0.05, 0.1, and 0.15 in percentages of population from 0 to 100%. We did not test higher levels of BAC because impacted agents could not move, since according to Table 3.1 people in such levels have several motor impairments and can even lose consciousness. As can be seen in Fig. 4.24 the simulation time is highly affected by increasing BAC level (black line has been used as reference for time obtained with non-affected population). Computing the average time obtained with BAC= 0.05

---

[13]http://extras.springer.com/.

[14]https://youtu.be/Eb6srKGnb5Y.

[15]http://www.who.int/.

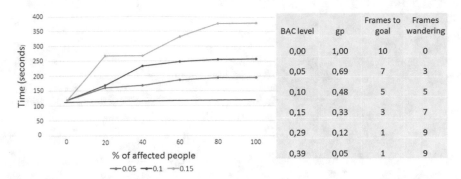

Fig. 4.24 Simulated data presenting the variation of evacuation time when BAC increases

for percentage from 20 to 100 of total population, we have a value 26% greater than when agents were homogeneous. For BAC= 0.1 and 0.15 the obtained values are respectively 62% and 127% greater than for homogeneous crowds.

As can be seen in Fig. 4.24 for BAC levels 0.05 and 0.1 simulation time is not highly impacted when 40% or more of the agents are affected by alcohol. This was not the expected behavior, but after many tests, we concluded that when almost half of the population is affected (uniformly distributed in the space), they disturb all agents (even the ones who are already affected), and consequently everybody takes more time to evacuate the environment. In addition, in Fig. 4.24 we can see the computed values gp_k, nf_k (frames keeping goal) and $f - nf_k$ (frames wandering) for agent k in certain BAC level. In these evaluations we considered $f = 10$ (as explained in Sect. 3.2.2). BAC levels of 0.29 and 0.39 have been simulated however a big part of agents could not leave the environment, so we could not measure the final time of simulation.

We were not able to compare virtual heterogeneous crowds with real life, since we do not have real data about BAC levels in real people. A contribution of this report in this aspect is the modeling of heterogeneous crowds based on alcohol literature. The results obtained by this project are published in Cassol et al. (2015).

4.6   Summary

This chapter discusses a set of case studies performed by CrowdSim. First of all, we have described the pipeline applied in all the performed case studies. Follow, each project was detailed, and presented a real application of crowd simulation in several fields. Different evaluations have been applied during the case studies performance, since statistical analysis as well as comparison of simulation results with real life data. In addition, 3D virtual world files and videos are available.

Chapter 5
Crowd Analysis Based on Computer Vision

5.1 Introduction

When evaluating or simulating crowd egress situations, there are several parameters that should be taken into account. For instance, the initial distribution of the people and/or local densities are important to assess possible hazardous events; tracking people or detecting main flows can be very useful to identify main escape routes or bottlenecks; finally, crowd behavior understanding methods can be used to identify collective behavior (e.g., groups) or unusual/abnormal events.

Collecting data from crowded scenes is a challenging task. Manual labeling is very time consuming and mostly undoable in real time. On the other hand, there are many automatic or semiautomatic methods for crowd analysis based on computer vision. In fact, there are several surveys on this topic published in different research fields such as disaster risk reduction (Yogameena and Nagananthini 2017) and crowd management (Grant and Flynn 2017; Li et al. 2015). Also, there has been significant work toward bridging the gap between crowd simulation and analysis, as reported in Zhan et al. (2008), Jacques et al. (2010).

Another important issue regarding the evaluation of computer vision techniques applied to crowded scenes is the availability of public datasets. As discussed in Li et al. (2015), Grant and Flynn (2017), there has been an increasing number of datasets containing crowded scenarios, suitable for a variety of applications. This part of the book will provide an overview of existing approaches for crowd analysis using computer vision, as well as validation and publicly available databases focusing on three main aspects: (i) people counting/density estimation; (ii) people tracking or estimation of main crowd flows; and (iii) behavior understanding, as illustrated in Fig. 5.1.

© Springer International Publishing AG 2017
V.J. Cassol et al., *Simulating Crowds in Egress Scenarios*,
https://doi.org/10.1007/978-3-319-65202-3_5

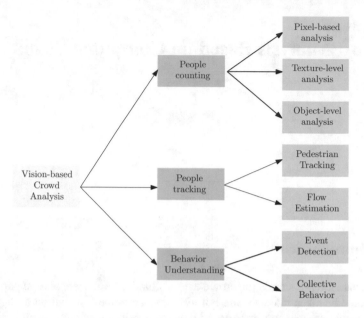

Fig. 5.1 Overview of the adopted taxonomy for vision-based crowd analysis methods

5.2   People Counting and Density Estimation

An important problem in crowd analysis is people counting and/or density estimation. For instance, the development of automatic, objective crowd counting algorithms can be used to resolve disputes over widely disagreeing attendance estimates in public events or protests. Also, crowd density analysis could be used to measure the comfort level in public spaces, or to detect potentially dangerous situations such as asphyxia by chest compression or stampeding at very high densities (Fruin 1971a), which is important in the context of crowd egress models. Typically, crowd counting methods try to locate each person (or body part, e.g., head) present in the scene, while density estimation methods provide a continuous map with the estimated local density, as illustrated in Fig. 5.2.

There are several models developed to estimate the number of people in crowded scenarios using computer vision techniques. In this work, we adopt the same taxonomy used in Jacques et al. (2010), and divide existing techniques into three categories: (i) pixel-based analysis, (ii) texture-based analysis, and (iii) object-level analysis. However, other taxonomies also exist. For instance, the survey paper (Ryan et al. 2015) categorizes crowd counting algorithms are generally into two groups: holistic and local.

Fig. 5.2 Illustration of pedestrian counting and density estimation. **a** Original frame from the UCF CC 50 dataset (Idrees et al. 2013). **b** Example of pedestrian counting (blue dots). **c** Example of density estimation

5.2.1 Pixel-Level Analysis

Pixel-based methods rely on very local features (such as individual pixel analysis obtained through background subtraction models or edge detection) to estimate the number of people in a scene. Since very low-level features are used, this class is mostly focused on density estimation rather than precise people counting.

The work described in Davies et al. (1995) was one of the pioneers to use computer vision techniques for obtaining automatically some kind of information from crowds. In their work, the authors proposed an approach to estimate the density of the crowd using pixel-level information. They combined a background subtraction technique and detected edges to estimate the density. They assumed linear models to map foreground pixels or edges to the number of people, which were integrated using a Kalman Filtering approach to improve the results. Their method also includes geometrical correction due to the perspective of the camera, to account for the fact that the dimension of the same person (in pixels) may change at different locations (the size in pixels decreases as the distance from the camera increases). Clearly, the linear function that maps pixel counts to the number of people in the scene fails when strong occlusions occur, which is common for lateral or oblique camera setups in denser crowds.

Regazzoni et al. (1993) proposed an approach to estimate the crowd density in images. In their work, features extracted from each acquired image (basically the results of an edge detection algorithm and finding vertical edges) are related to the number of people present in the monitored scene by using nonlinear models obtained by means of Dynamic Programming in an off-line training phase. In the operation phase, the detected features are integrated across time through an Extended Kalman Filter to improve the results. Although they had shown improvement over a competitive approach based on Belief Bayesian Networks (Ottonello et al. 1992), their method was mostly focused on indoor scenes with a limited number of people (up to around 30). Furthermore, the off-line training procedure is adjusted to a given camera setup and scenario, and changes require a new training phase.

Cho et al. (1999) presented a method based on neural networks to estimate the crowd density in subway stations. Their objective was to detect high density situations and to provide statistical analysis about the flow of people across time for activity planning. They proposed a simple edge detector based on binary image thresholding, and explored the length of detected edges as a feature for people counting through a single hidden layer neural network. Their approach was implemented using a hybrid method for global learning that combines the least-squares method with 3 types of global optimization approaches, defined as follow: (i) Random Search, (ii) Simulated Annealing, and (iii) Genetic Algorithms. Their results presented approximately 90% of correctness over all tested methods. They also pointed out that the combination of least-square and random search algorithm was the fastest, opposed to the combination of the least-square and simulated annealing (about 100 times slower).

Yang et al. (2003) proposed a multi-camera-based method to segment people and to estimate the number of people in crowded video sequences. In their work, groups of image sensors were used to segment foreground objects from the background, aggregate the resulting silhouettes over a network, and compute a planar projection of the scene's visual hull. An advantage of their approach is that the system does not compute any feature correspondences across views. Thus, the computation cost increases linearly with the number of cameras. Instead, the authors introduce a geometric algorithm that computes bounds on the number and possible locations of people using silhouettes obtained by each sensor through background subtraction, in each region of the projection. However, in very crowded situations some objects may be completely hidden from all views and therefore impossible to localize individually.

Ma et al. (2004) proposed a crowd density estimation algorithm for surveillance purposes. In their work, an approach based on pixel counting of foreground objects is used to estimate the crowd density, combined with a projective correction using a calibrated camera. A linear relation between the number of pixels and number of persons was then derived by applying the geometric correction. The density over time is also monitored, aiming to detect some unusual behavior. Their approach suffers the same occlusion problems faced in Davies et al. (1995), since a linear model is used to estimate the people count.

Kong et al. (2006) presented a method based on learning to estimate the number of people in crowds. Edge orientation and the histogram of the object areas (extracted from foreground objects through a background subtraction algorithm) are used as image features. A normalization procedure is performed to account for camera perspective, and the training model used to relate the detected features with the number of people was based on a feed-forward neural network. An interesting characteristic of this approach is the training of normalized features, so that changes in the camera setup do not require a new training phase.

Recently, techniques based on deep learning have gained increased attention. Although they are pixel-based by nature, since the raw pixel values are used as input, the convolutions typically used in the initial layers explore local information as well. In Zhang et al. (2016b), the authors devise a convolutional neural network (CNN) that takes as input the image and outputs a local density maps (people per square meter). To cope with different head sizes on the same image, caused by perspective distortion, the authors proposed the use of filters with different sizes of local receptive field to learn the map from the raw pixels to the density maps. To obtain the crowd count, the density map is integrated.

5.2.2 Texture Analysis

Algorithms that rely on texture analysis explore a coarser grain if compared to pixel-based methods, as texture modeling requires the analysis of image patches. Although this class of methods explores higher level features when compared to pixel-based approaches, it is also mostly used to estimate the number of people in a scene rather than identifying individuals.

Marana et al. (1998) analyzed four methods used in texture analysis and three classifiers to deal with the crowd density estimation problem. Regarding texture analysis, they compared the following 4 methods: gray-level dependence matrix, straight lines segments, fourier analysis, and fractal dimension. Regarding the classifiers, they compared the following 3 methods: neural network, statistics (Bayesian) and a fitting function-based approach. They found better results when using the gray-level dependence matrix-based method, providing better contrast and homogeneity as texture features, combined with a Bayesian classifier. However, it should be noted that they generated ground truth information empirically, which could affect the comparison. They estimated the crowd density in one of the five following classes: very low density, low density, moderate density, high density, and very high density. The authors mentioned that the method cannot discriminate very well the difference between high and very high densities.

Wu et al. (2006) proposed an approach to estimate the crowd density using Support Vector Machines (SVMs) and texture analysis. In their work, a perspective projection model is adopted to generate a series of multi-resolution cells, and the gray-evel dependence matrix method is used to extract textural information within these cells. A multi-scale texture vector is built, and a SVM is trained to relate the textural features with the actual density of the scene. The authors reported a maximum estimation error for each cell below 5%, and proposed as future work the possibility of including a background subtraction method in the feature extraction stage. One drawback of their approach, however, is the need of retraining the SVM for scenarios with different camera setups, since the density cells are highly dependent on camera parameters.

Rahmalan et al. (2006) made a comparison of three techniques used in texture analysis to tackle the crowd density estimation problem. The three analyzed techniques were the gray-level dependence matrix, the Minkowski fractal dimension, and a third one named translation-invariant orthonormal Chebyshev moments. The extracted features are classified in a neural network (self-organizing maps), and their analysis indicates that the method based on the Minkowski dimension presented the worst results, whilst the translation-invariant orthonormal Chebyshev moments had the best overall results. However, they found a small difference between the translation-invariant orthonormal Chebyshev moments method and the gray-level dependence matrix method, indicating that it should be better investigated in a future work.

Chan et al. (2008) developed a crowd counting algorithm based on a texture-based motion segmentation technique and Gaussian process regression. The authors initially segment the crowd into different motion directions using the mixture of dynamic textures, and for each motion cluster they extract segment features (area, perimeter, perimeter edge orientation, perimeter–area ratio), internal edge features (total edge pixels, edge orientation, Minkowski dimension) and texture features (homogeneity, energy, and entropy). These features are normalized to account for camera perspective, and a Gaussian process regression is used to relate the number of people per segment. Chan and Vasconcelos (2009) explored a similar idea, but using Bayesian–Poisson regression instead (which is more adequate for discrete processes, such as people counting). The regression used in both papers presented good results, but they are dependent on the segmentation step, which may fail for unstructured crowds with erroneous motion.

Chan and Vasconcelos (2012) presented an approach for estimating the size of inhomogeneous crowds based on video sequences. The crowd is initially segmented into components of homogeneous motion based on a dynamic-texture motion model. A set of holistic low-level features is extracted from each segmented region, and a function that maps features into estimates of the number of people per segment is learned using two Bayesian regression models: a combination of Gaussian process regression with a compound kernel (GPR), and Bayesian treatment of Poisson regression (BPR). They reported that BPR was more accurate for denser crowds, whereas GPR performed better when the crowd was less dense. It is important to point out that their approach is view-dependent, since training and test samples are acquired from the same (fixed) camera.

5.2.3   Object-Level Analysis

Methods that rely on object level analysis try to identify individual objects in a scene. In the context of crowd counting, that means detecting pedestrians (whole bodies or parts, such as heads) in images or video sequences. They tend to produce more accurate results when compared to pixel-level analysis or texture-based approaches, but identifying individuals is mostly feasible in lower density crowds. In denser crowds, clutter and severe occlusions make the individual counting problem almost impossible to solve, despite the recent advances of computer vision and pattern recognition techniques. In fact, there are several approaches for the generic problem of pedestrian detection (in either sparser or denser situations), and a recent popular survey paper was presented by Dollar and colleagues (Dollar et al. 2012). The remaining of this section will focus on approaches tailored for crowded scenes.

Lin et al. (2001) proposed an algorithm to estimate the crowd density in three stages. In the first one, they searched for objects with head-like contour in the image space, using the Haar wavelet transform. In a second stage, the features of the object are analyzed, using a support vector machine, aiming to classify it as a head or not. Finally, a perspective transformation is done aiming better estimate the density of the entire crowd.

Zhao and Nevatia (2003) proposed a Bayesian approach to segment people in crowds. In their work, several 3D human models are used to represent the foreground objects in the scene, and a probabilistic model based on Markov Chain Monte Carlo (MCMM) integrates in a Bayesian framework the tracked features, like body shape, people height, camera model, head candidates, foreground objects, for example. However, in high density crowds, the full body representation is usually not very useful, as severe occlusions tend to hide most of the body (and part of the head).

Leibe et al. (2005) proposed a pedestrian detection scheme using a top-down segmentation approach. In fact, they explore a combination of local features (a scale-invariant version of the Implicit Shape Model) and global features (Chamfer distance) to obtain the probability of a person being present, which is measured by comparing small learned image patches of the appearance of humans and their occurrence distribution. Their algorithm can reliably detect and localize pedestrians in relatively crowded scenes and with severe overlaps. However, the lateral camera setup explored in Leibe and Schiele (2005) generates too many occlusions (partial or total) in very crowded scenes, which cannot be handled adequately in such scenarios.

Rittscher et al. (2005) proposed an algorithm for segmenting human figures in video sequences. They try to fit multiple object hypotheses to explain the occurrence of a set of image features, dealing with occlusions by computing joint image likelihood of multiple objects. The image features are based on the contours of segmented foreground objects, assuming that foreground blobs are available. The joint likelihood is then obtained using the Expectation-Maximization (EM) algorithm. It is interesting to note that explicit camera information is used in Rittsche et al. (2005), which makes the approach suitable for a variety of camera setups. On the other hand, the performance of their approach is highly dependent on the extraction of foreground blobs that generate the image features.

Rabaud and Belongie (2006) presented a method to segment individuals in a crowd. They use a feature tracking algorithm, namely the KLT (Kanade–Lucas–Tomasi) tracker, to detect moving objects in the scene. The tracker is then combined with a temporal and a spatial filter, and a clustering algorithm is used to group similar features into a trajectory, which is related to a single object. The authors validated their results using 3 datasets, containing ground truth information generated by a specialist. They also use a video sequence with a crowd of cells, aiming to demonstrate the robustness of the proposed approach to segment individuals in crowds of different entities, but homogeneous among themselves. One clear limitation of this approach relates to stationary crowds, where motion information cannot be explored.

Brostow and Cipolla (2006) presented an unsupervised Bayesian clustering method to detect independent movements in a crowd. Their hypothesis is that a pair of points that move together should be part of the same entity. An optical flow algorithm combined with an exhaustive search (the search region is defined by ground-plane camera calibration) based on the normalized cross correlation is used to track some image features. An unsupervised Bayesian clustering algorithm then is applied to group such features, aiming to identify each individual moving in the crowd. An interesting characteristic of Brostow and Cipolla (2006) is that it does not require any training stage or appearance model to track individuals. However, since rigid motion is assumed, the algorithm may fail if strong arm movements are present.

Jones and Snow (2008) developed a classifier to detect pedestrians using spatiotemporal information. Their classifier involves three types of features: Haar-like features applied directly at each frame, absolute difference of Haar-like features in adjacent frames, and a shifted difference filter that aims to capture the motion of the pedestrians (8 shifting directions were used). Adaboost is then used to build a soft cascade classifier based on a set of manually labeled training images (in fact, eight classifiers were trained to deal with eight different motion directions). Their approach seems to successfully differentiate pedestrians from vehicles, but tends to fail for relatively dense scenarios. Also, it should be noted that changes in the camera setup that monitors the scene require a new training procedure, since the appearance of pedestrians trained with Adaboost depends on the positioning of the camera.

Idress et al. (2013) presented a crowd counting algorithm suited for extremely dense scenarios. Their approach is not solely based on objects, but it starts by counting heads within image patches using the Deformable Parts Model (Felzenszwalb et al. 2008) trained on INRIA Person dataset, and applied only the filter corresponding to head to the images. Assuming that packed crowds present a repetitive nature, they explore a Fourier-based method to obtain a second count. Finally, they obtain SIFT features within the patches and cluster them into a codebook, using support vector regression to obtain a third count estimates. These three estimates are then fused using a multi-scale Markov random Field.

A recent trend in machine learning and computer vision is the use of deep learning techniques. Stewart et al. (2016) presented an end-to-end people detection approach for crowded scenarios using Long-Short Term Memory (LSTM) networks. The main novelty introduced in Stewart et al. (2016) was the development of a trainable approach that jointly predicts the objects in an image using a loss function for sets of objects that combines elements of localization and detection.

5.2.4 Datasets and Validation

As noted in Ryan et al. (2015), crowd counting algorithms are evaluated using three criteria: mean absolute error (MAE), the root mean square error (RMSE) and mean relative error (MRE). These metrics are commonly used within the field for evaluating system performance. If a validation set containing N images is used, and $x_i, \hat{x}_i$ denote the actual and estimated number of people at frame i, respectively, then these metrics are computed as:

$$\text{MAE} = \frac{1}{N} \sum_{i=1}^{N} |x_i - \hat{x}_i|, \qquad (5.1)$$

$$\text{MRE} = \frac{1}{N} \sum_{i=1}^{N} \frac{|x_i - \hat{x}_i|}{x_i}, \tag{5.2}$$

$$\text{RMSE} = \sqrt{\frac{1}{N} \sum_{i=1}^{N} (x_i - \hat{x}_i)^2}. \tag{5.3}$$

The MAE provides an estimate of the absolute errors, and its interpretation should be done together with the number of people in analyzed frames. The RMSE presents a similar metric, but more sensible to larger errors due to the quadratic distance term. The MRE provides a relative error, and it already accounts for the number of people in the analyzed frames.

Also, it is important to note that there are several publicly available datasets for crowd counting/density estimation, with varying resolutions and density levels. These datasets have been gaining significant importance after the popularization of deep networks in the 2010s. These methods have improved the state of the art in many computer vision and pattern classification problems (LeCun et al. 2015), but typically require a large amount of training data.

The UCSD dataset was introduced in Chan et al. (2008), containing 2000 frames (200 s of a video sequence shot with a stationary camera) with 158×238 resolution, ranging from 11 to 46 pedestrians. The UCF CC 50 dataset (Idrees et al. 2013) contains fifty crowd images with varying resolutions and 64 K annotated humans, with the head counts ranging from 94 to 4543, and average of 1280 individuals per image. The scenes in these images also belong to a diverse set of events: concerts, protests, stadiums, marathons, and pilgrimages. The WorldExpo10 dataset was introduced in Zhang et al. (2015) and described in Zhang et al. (2016a), containing 1132 annotated video sequences captured by 108 surveillance cameras, all from Shanghai 2010 WorldExpo. It provides a total of 199,923 labeled pedestrians at the centers of their heads distributed in 3980 frames, which were uniformly sampled from all the video sequences, ranging from 1 to 253 pedestrians. Finally, the Shanghaitech dataset (2016b) contains 1198 annotated images, with a total of 330,165 people with centers of their heads annotated. It is divided into two parts: there are 482 images in Part A, created with images randomly crawled from the Internet, and 716 images in Part B, with images taken from the busy streets of metropolitan areas in Shanghai. Considering the two parts, crowd counts per image range from 9 to 3139.

5.3 Tracking

Another important problem related to crowd analysis is people tracking, which consists of identifying the position of the same person in a sequence of frames. The knowledge of individual trajectories in a crowd can be explored to identify main flows of a crowd, to locate entry and exit points in a filmed scenario, or to detect

(a)   (b)   (c)

Fig. 5.3 Illustration of pedestrian tracking and main flow estimation. **a** Frame from the PETS 2009 dataset and tracked pedestrians using (Führ and Jung 2014). **b** Frame from the UCF CC 50 dataset (Idrees et al. 2013) and **c** main flows obtained using a typical optical flow algorithm (Brox and Malik 2011)

abnormal motion behaviors. Although there are several approaches for the generic problem of object tracking, there are some particular characteristics when dealing with humans and crowds. People tend to walk on the ground plane in an upright pose and the upper body can be considered mostly a rigid object, which leads to specialized trackers (the problem is usually called pedestrian tracking). As the number of people (as well as the density) increases, it becomes progressively harder to identify and track each individual in the crowd. In such cases, an alternative solution is to obtain the main (local or global) flows of the crowd, as mentioned in Zhan et al. (2008); Jacques et al. (2010). Examples of multiple pedestrian tracking and main flows estimation are illustrated in Fig. 5.3.

In fact, there are two main approaches for crowd behavior analysis presented in Mehran et al. (2009): in the "object-based" approach, a crowd is treated as a collection of individuals. On the other hand, "holistic" approaches treat the crowd as a single entity, without the need of segmenting each individual. Individual pedestrian trackers are more adequate for the former approach, while optical flow methods are better suited for the latter one. It is also interesting to note that the problems of people counting and tracking are related, since both of them have the goal of identifying the participants of a crowd. However, the counting problem usually requires only an estimate of the number of people, regardless of their position (and temporal evolution). The tracking problem, on the other hand, involves the determination of the position of each person in the scene as a function of time. Nevertheless, object-based approaches for people counting can be used to initialize tracking algorithms, or even extended to perform both people counting and tracking.

The next sections will describe some approaches that either aim at tracking individuals or obtain the main (local or global) flows of a crowd. In general, the first class of methods is more adequate for sparse crowds, while the second on is typically used in denser scenarios.

5.3.1   Multiple Pedestrian Tracking

There are several methods for multiple pedestrian tracking, and many approaches have been presented in the past years. For example, Enzweiler and Gavrila presented a nice survey of pedestrian trackers using monocular cameras (Enzweiler and Gavrila 2009), while a comprehensive review and taxonomy of general 2D and 3D tracking algorithms were presented in Yilmaz et al. (2006), Lepetit and Fua (2005). More recently, Smeulders and colleagues presented a comprehensive (Smeulders et al. 2014) review of visual trackers, although not focusing specifically on pedestrians.

The available literature on the subject is extensive, and methods may vary w.r.t. the number of cameras (single or multiple), fixed or moving camera(s), fusion of other modalities (e.g. depth information or cell phone signals). This brief review will focus mostly on tracking methods that rely on single, static cameras.

One of the first proposed systems for pedestrian tracking was the W4 algorithm (Haritaoglu et al. 1998). It employed background segmentation combined with shape and texture information to perform real time tracking in grayscale video sequences. Fleuret et al. (2008) also explored background segmentation coupled with appearance models built using color histograms.

A challenging aspect of pedestrian tracking is to maintain a good localization during and after an occlusion. A simple way to deal with partial occlusions is to consider the target object as a set of patches. The rationale behind this idea is that if some patches are occluded and tracked incorrectly, the remaining patches can provide a good estimate of the pose. The FragTrack algorithm (Adam et al. 2006) divides the target region into multiple image fragments at initialization. For each fragment, a vote map is constructed using image histograms. Then, these maps are combined in a robust way so that the influence of outliers is reduced. Dihl et al. (2011) also use the same idea for object tracking, but track each patch independently and combine these tracking results to estimate the location of the target. The use of multiple fragments has shown good results in generic tracking applications (Adam et al. 2006; Dihl et al. 2011), and also when tailored to pedestrian tracking (Führ and Jung 2012, 2014). For instance, Führ and Jung (2014) presented a patch-based multiple pedestrian tracker using static calibrated cameras. In their approach, a pedestrian detector is applied to initialize the targets, which are validated using background removal. A set of vertical patches (in the world coordinate system) is then used to represent each pedestrian. They are tracked independently, and combined in a robust manner using weighted vector median filters assuming motion parallel to the ground plane (Fig. 5.4).

A different class of approaches for pedestrian tracking is based on the concept of tracking-by-detection. These methods are based on the continuous application of a detection algorithm in individual frames, and then performing the association of detection results across frames. Benfold and Reid (2011) use Histograms of Oriented Gradients (HoGs) (Dalal and Triggs 2005) and Kanade–Lucas–Tomasi (KLT) tracking to detect people and estimate their motion between detections. To obtain the final trajectories, a Markov Chain Monte Carlo data association is applied within a temporal window. Pirsiavash et al. (2011) proposed a method that first detects all the pedestrians in the sequence and then uses dynamic programming to associate the detections into trajectories. Methods that performed data association globally (Pirsiavash et al. 2011) or within a sliding-window (Fagot-Bouquet et al. 2016; Benfold and Reid 2011) perform generally well, since looking at future frames can reduce uncertainty at current and past times. Yet, this comes with a price: the latency caused

(a)   (b)

(c)   (d)

Fig. 5.4 Overview of the multiple pedestrian tracker in Führ and Jung (2014). **a** Pedestrian detection. **b** Background subtraction. **c** Pedestrian validation and main axis detection. **d** Patch distribution

by the use of future observations in the estimation of the current state, i.e., they are not causal.

A hybrid approach was presented in Babaee et al. (2016). Instead of tracking objects (detection boxes) or individual pixels (optical flow), they deal with superpixels (since the superpixels are extracted from detection boxes, this method was categorized as a multiple pedestrian tracker and not as crowd flow estimation). Based on the extracted superpixels, they build a flow graph that encodes segmentation, reconstruction, and tracking of superpixels.

When dealing with denser crowds, some tracking approaches also explore crowd simulation models to take into account people interactions and predict local motion patterns. In Bera et al. (2016), a set of crowd videos is used to learn the motion model parameters used in a particle filter. More precisely, the motion model is based on the Reciprocal Velocity Obstacles (RVO) (2008), which is a motion model for local collision avoidance and navigation. Despite the promising results shown in Bera et al. (2016), target initialization is still a challenge in denser crowds. Alahi et al. (2016) presented an approach that tackles the problem of trajectory prediction as a sequence generation task, where we are interested in predicting the future trajectory of people based on their past positions. Then, they proposed an LSTM model that can learn general human movement using a training dataset, and predict their future trajectories.

5.3.2 Crowd Flow Estimation

Crowd flow estimation methods extract local or global motion patterns in a crowd. The local flows can be estimated using individual pedestrian tracks, as described in Sect. 5.3.1, using tracklets obtained with sparse feature trackers, or using optical flow methods. This section focuses on approaches based on tracklets and optical flow methods.

The people counting approach described in Rittsche et al. (2005) also presented an extension for tracking. In their approach, each track is modeled by a color signature, an appearance template and a probabilistic target mask that is an autoregressive estimate of the foreground information. People walking close to each other are clustered into "group tracks", and individual tracks within the same group are smoothed using a constant velocity Kalman filter. Their approach can handle short term occlusions between isolated tracks, but it tends to fail when the crowd density gets very high.

Ali and Shah (2008) proposed an approach for people tracking in structured high density scenarios. In their approach, each frame of a video sequence is divided into cells, each cell presenting just one particle. A person consists of a set of particles, and each person is affected by the layout of the scene (obstacles and barriers, which are learned automatically), as well as the motion of other people. An interesting aspect of this work is the use of concepts related to crowd modeling (obstacles and relationship with neighbors). On the other hand, since a manual identification of the individuals is required to initialize each track, this approach is not adequate for automatic people counting. Furthermore, since the cells used for tracking have fixed size, problems may arise in the far field of oblique cameras.

Rodriguez et al. (2009) presented a tracking approach to deal with unstructured environments, in which the motion of a crowd appears to be random with different participants moving in different directions over time (e.g. a crossway). They employ the Correlated Topic Model (CTM), which allows each location of the scene to have various crowd behaviors. In their approach, the video sequence is divided into non-overlapping clips. For each of these clips, the optical flow is computed, and both position and velocity vector are quantized to generate a word in a codebook, needed for the CTM. The motion words are assumed to arise from a generative process, whose parameters are estimated using a collection of training video sequences. Their approach is indeed able to deal with very dense crowds, but as the approach described in Ali and Shah (2008), there is the issue of track initialization.

Kratz and Nishino (2012) introduced a crowd motion model that encodes the temporal evolution of local motion patterns represented with directional statistics distributions, by using a collection of hidden Markov models (HMMs). The proposed model is able to encode temporally varying multi-modal flows in the image space, and it is also explored to predict the desired motion pattern of individuals.

Zhao et al. (2012) presented an approach that explores main crowd flows to perform single or multiple object tracking. They initially use the KLT tracker to obtain short tracklets, obtaining 4D manifolds formed by position (x, y) and speed (v_x, v_y) coordinates. Such manifolds, which embed information about the local crowd flows, are combined with appearance models for multiple pedestrian tracking. Zhou et al. (2013) also explored particle tracking using KLT, and proposed a collectiveness measure to evaluate the degree of individuals acting as a union in collective motion. The proposed measure can be applied to identify local flows that arise in group walking, lane formation, and different traffic modes, for instance. Fradi et al. (2017) also explored tracklets from sparsely tracked features, and modeled their spatial interactions using Delaunay triangulations. Then, graph clustering can be used to identify local flows with coherent motion.

Wang et al. (2014) presented an approach for detecting coherent motion in crowd scenes. Their main idea is to extract the optical flow from the scene, and then apply a coarse-to-fine thermal diffusion process to transfer the input motion field into a thermal energy field, generating a more accurate coherent motion field.

5.3.3   Datasets and Validation

There are many datasets and evaluation protocols for the problem of multiple pedestrian tracking in sparse or moderately dense scenes. One of the most popular is the PETS dataset (Ferryman and Ellis 2010), which contains a variety of multiple-view shots of different scenes, focusing mostly on surveillance applications. The MOTChallenge dataset (Leal-Taixé et al. 2015; Milan et al. 2016) is a compilation of several video sequences with annotated pixel or world coordinates (when some kind of camera calibration is available), available at https://motchallenge.net/. The Crowds-by-Example dataset (Lerner et al. 2007) presents four video sequences with a mostly top-view camera setup, shot at three different scenarios, along with the trajectories of the filmed people.

For the problem of multiple object tracking (MOT), a popular evaluation protocol is based on the *CLEAR MOT* metrics proposed in Bernardin and Stiefelhagen (2008). More precisely, they proposed a Multiple Object Precision Metric (MOTP), defined as

$$\text{MOTP} = \frac{\sum_{i,t} d_t^i}{\sum_t c_t},$$ (5.4)

where d_t^i is the distance from the ith object to the tracker hypothesis, and c_t is the number of matches found for time t. Hence, MOTP is the cumulative error is the estimated positions, so that lower values are expected in better trackers.

Along with MOTP, the authors in Bernardin and Stiefelhagen (2008) also proposed the Multiple Object Tracking Accuracy (MOTA), given by

$$\text{MOTA} = 1 - \frac{\sum_t (m_t + fp_t + mme_t)}{\sum_t g_t},$$ (5.5)

where m_t, fp_t, mme_t, and g_t are number of misses, of false positives, of mismatches, and total number of objects, respectively, for time t. The MOTA accounts for all object configuration errors made by the tracker, false positives, misses, mismatches, over all frames, and produces the largest possible value 1 (or 100%) when all the errors are zero.

Wu and Nevatia (2006) proposed to evaluate the performance of multi-object tracking algorithms using five criteria: number of "mostly tracked" trajectories (more than 80% of the trajectory is tracked), number of "mostly lost" trajectories (more than 80% of the trajectory is lost), number of "fragments" of trajectories (a result trajectory which is less than 80% of a ground truth trajectory), number of false trajectories (a result trajectory corresponding to no real object), and the frequency of identity switches (identity exchanges between a pair of result trajectories).

When dealing with crowd flows instead of individual pedestrian tracking, there are a few datasets depicting dense scenarios. The Data-driven Crowd Analysis dataset (Rodriguez et al. 2011) was constructed by crawling and downloading videos from search engines and stock footage websites, also containing ground-truth trajectories for 100 individuals (selected randomly from the set of all moving people). Image frames vary in resolution from 480×360 to 640×360. The Crowd Segmentation dataset (Ali and Shah 2007) contains videos of crowds and other high density moving objects, collected mainly from the BBC Motion Gallery and Getty Images website. In particular, the sequences related to human crowds depict situations such as marathons, entrance/exit in bus/train stations and busy pedestrian crossings, and are mostly low-resolution (480×360). The CUHK Crowd Dataset (Shao et al. 2014, 2016) contains 474 video clips from 215 crowded scenes, with a variety of image resolutions (from 360×480 to 1080×1920) and sequence lengths (from 100 to 200 frames in average). It also contains the ground truth information about the trajectories of some pedestrians.

Although the datasets described so far do present crowded scenarios (and some of them information about individual paths), they do not provide pixel-level information about the optical flow computed between adjacent frames of the video sequences. One way to overcome this limitation is through the use of crowd simulation algorithms, which can be used to generate realistic video sequences (if adequate rendering is performed) and at the same time having full control on the motion of the agents and ground truth information. For instance, the Agoraset dataset (Courty et al. 2014) is composed of eight synthetic scenes for which the positions of the agents are known.

Regarding the evaluation of main crowd flows, one possible strategy for quantitative evaluation is to use popular techniques defined to compare optical flow methods. In particular, the Middlebury evaluation strategy (Baker et al. 2011) consolidates a set of metrics to compare vector fields related to optical flows. Given estimated and actual flow vectors for one particular pixel p, given by (u, v) and (u_{gt}, v_{gt}), respectively, the Angular Error (AE) and Endpoint Error (EE) are given by

$$AE = \cos^{-1}\left(\frac{1 + uu_{gt} + vv_{gt}}{\sqrt{1 + u^2 + v^2}\sqrt{1 + u_{gt}^2 + v_{gt}^2}}\right), \tag{5.6}$$

$$EE = \sqrt{(u - u_{gt}^2) + (v - v_{gt})^2}. \tag{5.7}$$

Based on either AE or EE computed at each pixel, global statistics are used to assess the overall quality of an optical flow method. In particular, the percentage of pixels R_X that have an error measure above X are proposed in Baker et al. (2011). Similarly, they propose an overall accuracy metric A_X, which is the accuracy of the error measure at the Xth percentile.

5.4 Behavior Understanding

There are several approaches for analyzing crowd behaviors using computer vision. One class of such approaches focuses on detecting unusual or abnormal behavior, which is important in surveillance and crowd egress applications. Other methods aim to extract higher level information about a crowd scene in normal situations, such as crowd collectiveness or grouping behaviors. Such data is also very important when dealing with egress situations, since people in group tend to stay together during an evacuation process, unlike individuals.

Figure 5.5 illustrates the two main classes of behavior understanding methods tackled in this book. Figure 5.5a shows an example of unusual crowd behavior detection based on social forces, as proposed in Mehran et al. (2009), and Fig. 5.5b shows an example of group detection in (moderately) crowded scenes based on proxemics (Solera et al. 2016).

(a)   **(b)**

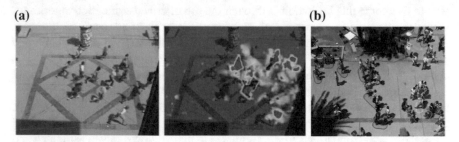

Fig. 5.5 Illustration of behavior-understanding models. **a** Example of unusual event detection in crowds using (Mehran et al. 2009). **b** Example of group detection using (Solera et al. 2016)

5.4.1 Unusual/Abnormal Event Detection

The main goal of unusual/abnormal event detection methods is to identify at which frames (when) an event occurred, and locate spatially (where) it happened. Those tasks can be accomplished by tracking individuals, but main flows are typically explored in denser crowds.

Motion histograms are popular in the context of unusual event detection in dense crowds. Dee and Caplier (2010) presented a prototype system for the automated analysis of crowded scenes based on local histograms of motion vectors. After detecting pedestrians and faces to estimate scale, they use the KLT tracker (Shi and Tomasi 1994) to obtain pieces of trajectories which are used to estimate local motion. Histograms of local motion are computed regionally by dividing each frame into a set of square regions, and comparing the histograms of each frame to the average histograms of a training set. Cong et al. (2011) used a multi-scale histogram of optical flow (MHOF) and introduced a sparse reconstruction cost (SRC) based on a set of training samples to measure the normality of a given video sequence. In the test phase, a high SRC value e implies a high reconstruction cost, and hence a high probability of being an abnormal sample. To achieve local abnormal detection, they explore local histograms computed at image patches. de Almeida et al. (2013) presented an approach for detecting global motion changes in crowded scenes. They obtain the crowd flow using optical flow algorithms, and estimate the flow in the world coordinate system using the ground plane homography. A 2D motion histogram based on speed and orientation is built, as illustrated in Fig. 5.6, and global changes are based on the comparison of those histograms within a temporal window.

Wu et al. (2014) presented an approach to detect escape behaviors in crowded scenes. They explored foreground pixel extraction and optical flow to characterize local crowd behavior, model escape and non-escape crowd behaviors in a Bayesian fashion, and detect escape behaviors using posterior probabilities. The results shown in their paper are promising, but it is limited to detecting only escape behaviors.

Kaltsa et al. (2015) also focused on the detection and localization of events in crowded scenes. In their method, histograms of oriented swarms were introduced to build a description of the scene, based on spatiotemporal volumes of the video sequence. Lee et al. (2015) proposed the use of *motion influence maps* to represent human activities. Such maps are able to characterize the movement speed, direction, and size of the objects or subjects and their interactions within a frame sequence, allowing the detection of global or localized events. Li et al. (2014) tackled the problem of localizing anomalous behaviors in crowds by proposing a spatiotemporal detector. Their approach is based on a video representation that accounts for both appearance and dynamics, using a mixture of dynamic texture models. Spatial and temporal anomaly maps are then defined at multiple spatial scales, by considering the scores of these operators at progressively larger regions of support, guaranteeing global consistency of detected events. Chong et al. (2014) used the Hierarchical Dirichlet Process (HDP) to cluster trajectories in different periods of the day, obtaining time-dependent Regions of Interest (ROIs). To detect global changes in the crowd

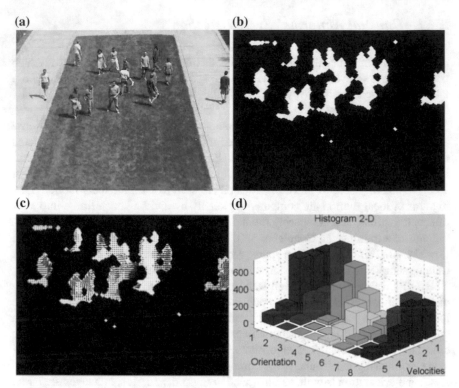

Fig. 5.6 Motion detection based on 2D histograms as proposed in de Almeida et al. (2017). **a** Example of input frame. **b** Foreground pixels. **c** Optical flow vectors at foreground pixels. **d** Surface illustrating the 2D orientation-speed histogram in the world coordinate system

behavior, speed-orientation histograms at different time periods are compared. Furthermore, a local analysis can be also performed within each of the learned ROIs.

Briassouli and Kompatsiaris (2011) presented an approach based on properties of the data in the Fourier domain for detecting new events in crowds. This method does not require extensive training, estimation of the optical flow, or data modeling; to do this they model the random crowd motion using the Fourier transform. New events are then identified through statistical change detection methods. Haque and Murshed (2010) presented a new approach for handling crowd scenarios that is based neither on motion cues nor trajectories. Instead, the explored feature extraction based on frame-set characteristics computed on foreground blobs. The temporal variation of frame-level features is analyzed over a sliding temporal window, and a set of specific events is trained using Support Vector Machines (SVMs).

Some methods explore theoretical models of crowd dynamics to detect events. Mehran et al. (2009) explored a Social Force Model (SFM) to detect and localize unusual behavior in crowded scenes. In their approach, the interaction of particles guided by a space–time average of the optical flow is estimated using a SFM, and a bag of features approach is adopted for unusual event detection. Since the bag of words method does not implicitly provide a method to localize the unlikely visual words, abnormalities in an abnormal frame are identified by locating the regions of high force flow. In Chen and Huang (2011), the optical flow was used to cluster human crowds into groups in an unsupervised manner using a novel approach called adjacency-matrix-based clustering (AMC). Each cluster is characterized based on the chosen SFM through a "dominant force", which guides the group. Unusual crowd events are detected when the orientation of a crowd is abruptly changed or when interactions within the crowd are not similar to the predicted value.

Zhou et al. (2012, 2015) proposed a new Mixture model of Dynamic pedestrian-Agents (MDA) to learn the collective behavior of pedestrians. The MDAs are learned based on a set of (possibly fragmented) tracks, and abnormal behaviors are detected by measuring the likelihoods of the trajectories with the MDA. Similarly to the MDAs in Zhou et al. (2012, 2015), the approach by Liu et al. (2014) is able to learn motion patterns in unstructured scenes by exploring visible entry and exit points. Based on these points, trajectories are clustered and outliers are detected as abnormal.

Some approaches adopt a physically based analysis of the flow to detect events. For example, the method presented by Wu et al. (2010) aims to detect and localize anomalies in complex and crowded sequences by using a Lagrangian particle dynamics approach, together with chaotic modeling. Also, representative trajectories are defined to serve as compact modeling elements in crowd flows. Such trajectories also provide a simple way of obtaining time series data, which can effectively be used for chaotic modeling of a scene. The representative chaotic feature set is regulated to reliably capture trajectory dynamics to be used for probabilistic anomaly detection and localization. Solmaz et al. (2012) explored concepts related to the stability of a dynamical system to detect pre-determined events in a crowd, based on the optical flow of the scene. An approach for crowd behavior modeling based on spatiotemporal viscous fluid fields was proposed by Su et al. (2013). The authors built a variation matrix computed using a spatiotemporal volume, and use the corresponding eigenvalues to describe the local fluctuation.

5.4.2 Collective Behavior Analysis

When individual pedestrian tracks are available, the spatiotemporal relationships between tracked pedestrians can be used to infer grouping information. In Jacques et al. (2007), an algorithm for group detection and classification as voluntary or involuntary based on interpersonal distances was proposed. Using a top-down camera, pedestrians are tracked and the underlying Voronoi Diagrams are used to quantify the sociological concept of proxemics and personal space (Hall 1959). The temporal evolution of the Voronoi Diagrams is used to identify groups in the scene, and the portion of the personal space within each individual's field of view is used to classify the groups as voluntary or involuntary. An example of group detection in Jacques et al. (2007) is show in Fig. 5.7. Solera et al. (2016) also explored the concept of proxemics to detect small social groups in crowds. More precisely, they infer peo-

(a)   (b)

(c)   (d)

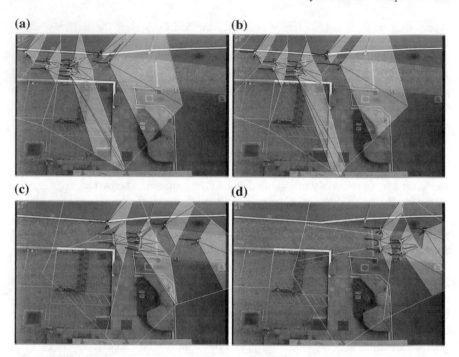

Fig. 5.7 Example of group detection in Jacques et al. (2007), where members within a group are connected by green lines

ple interactions based on distances and explore the econometric parameter Granger causality (Granger 1969) to measure to what extent pedestrians are mutually affecting their motion paths, leading to an intermediate representation between individuals and the whole crowd.

Other social models have also been explored for collective behavior analysis. Cristani et al. (2011) explored the concept of F-formations, which was introduced in Kendon (1977) and mostly characterizes the shapes of static groups of people. Since orientational information is required in the F-formation definition, the authors introduce a probabilistic approach that models the head orientations obtained with vision algorithms as random variables following a 2D Gaussian distribution to account for uncertainty. Ge et al. (2012) proposed a method to discover pedestrian groups in a video sequence inspired by the sociological work of McPhail and Wohlstein (1982). First, they combine a pedestrian detector, a particle filter for tracking and a data association scheme to merge people tracklets into trajectories. These trajectories are projected onto the ground plane using a homography, and a hierarchical clustering approach is used to identify and merge/split small groups of people.

Cheng et al. (2014) represented the problem of group activity recognition at multiple levels: individual, pairwise and larger groups. Based on the location of detected pedestrians, the Delaunay triangulation algorithm is applied to the polygon that connects the people in the scene. They then explore the areas, edges and centers of the

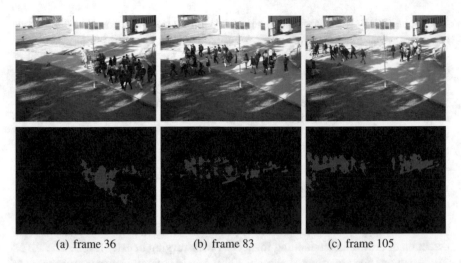

(a) frame 36   (b) frame 83   (c) frame 105

Fig. 5.8 Example of group splitting with de Almeida et al. (2017), using the PETS2009 S3. Event Recognition dataset, sequence 3

circumcircles of all triangles within the Delaunay triangulation to represent the group compactness from a global perspective.

Feng and Banhu (2015) proposed a method to identify groups and their interactions using what they called an Evolving Tracklet Interaction Network (ETIN). Tracklets are considered as nodes in a graph and the edges represent the relation between different persons in the scene. The weight of these relations is measured by the weighted sum of aggregated positional, velocity and directional distances. Social groups are identified by maximizing the modularity of the network created using the tracklets that appear in a given period of time (snapshot).

de Almeida et al. (2017) presented an extension of Almeida and Jung (2013) to identify main "groups", and also motion changes within each detected group. The core idea is to segment the crowd flow, estimated in the world coordinate system, which are defined as sets of people (pixels) having coherent motion vectors and spatial proximity. The temporal histogram comparison used in Almeida and Jung (2013) is then applied to each detected group. Their method can also detect inter-group events, such as merging and splitting, as illustrated in Fig. 5.8. To generate a set of controlled environment with known information about events and groups, they also explored synthetic video sequences obtained with a crowd simulator.

Zhou et al. (2013) explored the concept of collectiveness in a crowd, using lower level tracking features (tracklet-based), which are more adequate for denser crowds. Their core idea is to measure the behavior consistency within neighborhoods of the crowd, by computing velocity correlations. This concept is then extended for larger regions by evaluating the paths that connect two points in the scene. The proposed measure is used to detect collective motion patterns, which correspond to a variety of behaviors, such as group walking, lane formation, and different traffic modes, which are of a great interest for further video analysis and scene understanding.

Shao et al. (2015) presented a deep network o jointly learn and combine appearance and motion features for crowd understanding. Their main contribution was the use of motion channels instead of frame sequences to infer group properties, such as collectiveness, stability, and conflict.

Yi et al. (2016) focused on the detection of stationary groups in crowded scenes, which are important to assess crowd flow efficiency in the case of and egress situation. More precisely, their goal is to produce a 3D stationary-time map in the spatiotemporal space for an input video sequence.

5.4.3   Datasets and Validation

There are some popular datasets used for change detection, abnormal/unusual event detection or crowd understanding for scenes with varying density levels. The PETS 2009 dataset (Ferryman and Shahrokni 2009) consists of multisensor sequences containing different crowd activities. It is actually composed by three subsets, focused on person count/density estimation, people tracking and flow analysis/event recognition. Each subset contains several sequences, and each sequence contains different views (4–8). Information about camera parameters (calibration) is also available in the dataset.

The University of Minnesota Unusual Crowd Activity dataset (of Minnesota Crowd Activity Dataset 2017) provides eleven video sequences collected from three different scenarios. Most videos present people walking in a normal situation, and suddenly running to leave the scene. The WWW Crowd Dataset (Shao et al. 2015) (Who do What at someWhere) is a comprehensive crowd dataset collecting videos from movies, surveillance and web. It covers 10,000 video sequences from 8257 crowded scenes, in a total of 8 million frames. Its labeling data contains 94 crowd attributes including places (Where), subjects (Who), and activities (Why).

In terms of validation, there is no standardized procedure when dealing with event detection or behavior recognition. However, for the problems of change detection or unusual behavior detection, a common validation strategy is to evaluate the number of false positives (detection of nonexisting events) and false negatives (misdetection of an existing event) considering all frames of a video sequence or dataset.

Since most approaches present some kind of "acceptance threshold" for event detection, results can be shown as Receiver Operating Characteristic (ROC) curves, obtained by plotting the true positive rate (TPR) of a given method against the false positive rate (FPR) at various threshold settings. When the threshold is relaxed, the TPR tends to increase, typically at the cost of also increasing the FPR. To obtain a single quantitative value from the ROC curve, the Area Under the ROC Curve (AUC) is also popular, and it is equivalent to the probability that the classifier will rank a randomly chosen positive instance higher than a randomly chosen negative instance (Fawcett 2006). For methods that also localize the detected event, a similar analysis can be performed by using a distance threshold to detect if an event was correctly detected or not.

Chapter 6
Final Remarks

People, when part of a crowd, are able to perform unusual behavior, which would not be performed by a single person (LeBon 1895). A crowd is a powerful entity and its understanding is very important, specially regarding safety issues. The understanding of crowd motion can provide enough information in order to map people features and behaviors that can influence, among other aspects, the crowd efficiency in a specific environment. In addition, find out the impact one individual has over the others can be extremely relevant in order to estimate people motion and maybe the occurrence of dangerous situations. These examples are discussed and analyzed in this book. In particular, the technologies behind the detection of motion and behavior in videos are discussed in Chap. 5.

Once we understand what is relevant and how it could be analyzed, we are able to simulate the evolution of virtual people and crowds. In general, for safety simulation, methods deal with simple individuals and focus the contribution on effective control of macroscopic crowds. By simulating crowds, engineers can change parameters and analyze the evolution of individuals into a specific environment, according to different circumstances and constraints. Furthermore, companies can save money and time when simulating and analyzing crowd behavior during buildings design phase. In addition, extreme situations can be simulated, analyzed, and used to find out possible real improvements while avoiding exposing real people to dangerous training situations. Discussions about challenges and solved problems in safety systems were presented in Sect. 2.1.2. Also, available technologies (Sect. 3.1) have been presented as reference to future users and researchers.

This book aimed to point out the advantages of egress process simulations in computer. In addition to present available crowd simulation technologies, we detailed a case study. We discussed CrowdSim, a framework developed by the authors of this book to simulate crowds in different situations during an evacuation process. The goal was to provide a detailed experience in controlling and parametrizing crowd simulators. CrowdSim was detailed and some files let available in Sect. 3.2.

© Springer International Publishing AG 2017
V.J. Cassol et al., *Simulating Crowds in Egress Scenarios*,
https://doi.org/10.1007/978-3-319-65202-3_6

If simulating is an useful tool, it can only has real value if the credibility of tool and process are validated in some way. Once we want to use simulation results to improve aspects in real life, this validation is an important issue, i.e., to discuss and validate the coherency on data computed by crowd simulators is extremely relevant. In this book, we presented performed evaluations of CrowdSim according to international guidelines (International Maritime Organization 2007) and recognized scientific approaches (Galea 1998). A set of tests have been performed in different categories aiming to check the accuracy of results computed by CrowdSim. Our framework have shown acceptable results in all the tested categories.

Considering CrowdSim as a validated tool, we have applied it on a set of case studies. We detailed the main case studies developed in a night club, a college building, and a school. The goal was to estimate the behavior of crowds in different scenarios, considering aspects of comfort and safety. In some of the projects, we had the opportunity to compare simulated data against information captured from real- life evacuation exercises. Specifically, the night club case study was considered substantial to CrowdSim validation and should be carefully reviewed. In particular, some files are available for readers who desire to use another crowd simulator and compare data in this environment. We believe details are enough to provide comparisons.

Therefore, such case study has allowed us to collect data from a real-life evacuation exercise. Indeed, safety engineers have used CrowdSim to define an evacuation plan to be used during the real evacuation exercise. The first defined evacuation plan, specified by the engineers, when simulated in CrowdSim, taken approximately 5 min. In addition, this first plan have shown some specific attention points that were observed by the safety team and new evacuation plans were proposed. Two of new plans, when simulated, predicted a evacuation process in 142 and 147 s, respectively. The best of them, considering the total time for evacuation, was then applied by the safety team during the night of the real exercise and make the real people leave the night club in 175 s. This aspect was considered a quantitative evidence about the accuracy of *CrowdSim* results and validates our research approach. Furthermore, other aspects were evaluated as density, speeds, etc., as discussed in the book.

In this book, we covered topics on crowd simulation specifically on emergency situations. We discussed the basis for simulation coming from human beings and the main challenge to keep connecting with real-life motion and behavior. This aspect keeps computer vision and simulation researchers with big and challenge demands in order to build techniques and evaluate them coherently. We presented current technologies and let available files for people who want to start in the area or test software. The chapters presenting CrowdSim and the case studies had the goal to describe real experiments using crowd simulators in real life. Again files and numbers are available. Finally, computer vision techniques have been presented dealing with relevant topics of detecting motion and behavior of people in real life. However, the transformation from quotidian behaviors to evacuation simulations keeps a relevant aspect in the presented techniques. That is, film and detect people in one situation to simulate in another context, and again using computer vision to evaluate all data. This is how the present is writing the history about behavior simulation. For the future, certainly the integration with other technologies can bring new ground to this challenge area.

References

Adam A, Rivlin E, Shimshoni I (2006) Robust fragments-based tracking using the integral histogram. IEEE conference on computer vision and pattern recognition 1:798–805

Adrion WR, Branstad MA, Cherniavsky JC (1982) Validation, verification, and testing of computer software. ACM Comput Surv 14(2):159–192. https://doi.org/10.1145/356876.356879. http://doi.acm.org/10.1145/356876.356879

Aik LE, Choon TW (2012) Simulating evacuations with obstacles using a modified dynamic cellular automata mode. J Appl Math

Alahi A, Goel K, Ramanathan V, Robicquet A, Fei-Fei L, Savarese S (2016) Social LSTM: Human trajectory prediction in crowded spaces. In: Proceedings of the IEEE conference on computer vision and pattern recognition, pp 961–971

Ali S, Shah M (2007) A lagrangian particle dynamics approach for crowd flow segmentation and stability analysis. In: IEEE conference on computer vision and pattern recognition, 2007. CVPR'07, IEEE, pp 1–6

Ali S, Shah M (2008) Floor fields for tracking in high density crowd scenes. In: Proceedings of the European conference on computer vision, pp II: 1–14

Almeida IRd, Jung CR (2013) Change detection in human crowds. In: 26th SIBGRAPI-conference on graphics, patterns and images (SIBGRAPI), 2013, IEEE, pp 63–69

Babaee M, You Y, Rigoll G (2016) Pixel level tracking of multiple targets in crowded environments. In: European conference on computer vision, Springer, pp 692–708

Baker S, Scharstein D, Lewis J, Roth S, Black MJ, Szeliski R (2011) A database and evaluation methodology for optical flow. Int J Comput Vision 92(1):1–31

Beizer B (1984) Software system testing and quality assurance. Electrical computer science and engineering, Van Nostrand Reinhold Company. http://books.google.com.br/books?id=zNAmAAAAMAAJ

Benfold B, Reid I (2011) Stable multi-target tracking in real-time surveillance video. In: IEEE conference on computer vision and pattern recognition, pp 3457–3464

Bera A, Kim S, Manocha D (2016) Online parameter learning for data-driven crowd simulation and content generation. Comput Graph 55:68–79

Berlonghi A (1995-02-01T00:00:00) Understanding and planning for different spectator crowds 18(4):239–247. https://doi.org/10.1016/0925-7535(94)00033-Y. http://www.ingentaconnect.com/content/els/09257535/1995/00000018/00000004/art00033

Bernardin K (2008) Stiefelhagen R (2008) Evaluating multiple object tracking performance: the clear mot metrics. EURASIP J Image Video Process 1:1–10

Berseth G, Kapadia M, Haworth B, Faloutsos P (2014) SteerFit: automated parameter fitting for steering algorithms. In: ACM SIGGRAPH/eurographics symposium on computer animation, ACM, New York, NY, USA, SCA '14

Berseth G, Kapadia M, Faloutsos P (2015a) Robust space-time footsteps for agent-based steering. Comput Animation Virtual Worlds

Berseth G, Usman M, Haworth B, Kapadia M, Faloutsos P (2015b) Environment optimization for crowd evacuation. Computer Animation and Virtual Worlds 26(3–4):377–386. https://doi.org/10.1002/cav.1652

Boatright CD, Kapadia M, Shapira JM, Badler NI (2014) Generating a multiplicity of policies for agent steering in crowd simulation. Computer Animation and Virtual Worlds. https://doi.org/10.1002/cav.1572

Braun A, Musse SR, Oliveira LPLd, Bodmann BEJ (2003) Modeling individual behaviors in crowd simulation. In: CASA '03: proceedings of the 16th international conference on computer animation and social agents (CASA 2003), IEEE Computer Society, Washington, DC, USA, p 143

Briassouli A, Kompatsiaris I (2011) Spatiotemporally localized new event detection in crowds. In: IEEE international conference on computer vision (ICCV workshops), IEEE, pp 928–933

Brostow GJ, Cipolla R (2006) Unsupervised bayesian detection of independent motion in crowds. In: Proceedings of the IEEE conference on computer vision and pattern recognition, Washington, DC, USA, pp 594–601

Brox T, Malik J (2011) Large displacement optical flow: descriptor matching in variational motion estimation. IEEE Trans Pattern Anal Mach Intell 33(3):500–513

Cassol VJ (2016) Crowdsim: a framework to estimate safety of egress performance in real life scenarios. PhD thesis, PUCRS—Pontifical Catholic University of Rio Grande do Sul, Porto Alegre, Brazil

Cassol VJ, Rodrigues RA, Carneiro LCC, Silva A, Musse SR (2012) Crowdsim: Uma ferramenta desenvolvida para simulação de multidões. In: I Workshop de Simulação Militar - SBGames2012

Cassol V, Dal Bianco CM, Carvalho A, Brasil J, Monteiro M, Musse SR (2015) An experience-based approach to simulate virtual crowd behaviors under the influence of alcohol. In: IVA'15: proceedings of the 15th international conference on intelligent virtual agents, Springer, Berlin, Heidelberg

Challenger CRM Rose; Clegg (2009) Understanding crowd behaviours: guidance and lessons identified. The Cabinet Office Emergency Planning College, York, UK

Chan AB, Vasconcelos N (2009) Bayesian poisson regression for crowd counting. In: Proceedings of IEEE international conference on computer vision, pp 1–7

Chan AB, Vasconcelos N (2012) Counting people with low-level features and bayesian regression. IEEE Trans Image Process 21(4):2160–2177

Chan A, Liang Z, Vasconcelos N (2008) Privacy preserving crowd monitoring: Counting people without people models or tracking. In: Proceedings of IEEE conference on computer vision and pattern recognition, pp 1–7

Chen DY, Huang PC (2011) Motion-based unusual event detection in human crowds. J Vis Commun Image Represent 22(2):178–186

Cheng Z, Qin L, Huang Q, Yan S, Tian Q (2014) Recognizing human group action by layered model with multiple cues. Neurocomputing

Cho SY, Chow TWS, Leung CT (1999) A neural-based crowd estimation by hybrid global learning algorithm. IEEE transactions on systems, man, and cybernetics 29(4):535–541

Chong X, Liu W, Huang P, Badler NI (2014) Hierarchical crowd analysis and anomaly detection. J Visual Lang Comput 25(4):376–393

Chu ML, Parigi P, Law K, Latombe JC (2014) Modeling social behaviors in an evacuation simulator. Computer Animation and Virtual Worlds 25(3–4):373–382. https://doi.org/10.1002/cav.1595

Cocking C, Drury J (2008) The mass psychology of disasters and emergency evacuations: a research report and implications for the fire and rescue service. Fire Saf Technol Manage 10(2):13–19. http://eprints.brighton.ac.uk/11416/

Cong Y, Yuan J, Liu J (2011) Sparse reconstruction cost for abnormal event detection. In: IEEE conference on computer vision and pattern recognition, IEEE, pp 3449–3456

Courty N, Allain P, Creusot C, Corpetti T (2014) Using the agoraset dataset: Assessing for the quality of crowd video analysis methods. Pattern Recogn Lett 44:161–170

Cristani M, Bazzani L, Paggetti G, Fossati A, Tosato D, Del Bue A, Menegaz G, Murino V (2011) Social interaction discovery by statistical analysis of f-formations. In: BMVC, vol 2, p 4

Curtis S, Best A, Manocha D (2016) Menge: a modular framework for simulating crowd movement. Collective Dyn 1:1–40. https://doi.org/10.17815/CD.2016.1. https://collective-dynamics. eu/index.php/cod/article/view/A1

Dalal N, Triggs B (2005) Histograms of oriented gradients for human detection. IEEE conference on computer vision and pattern recognition 1:886–893

Davies AC, Yin JH, Velastin SA (1995) Crowd monitoring using image processing. IEE Electron Commun Eng J 37–47

de Almeida IR, Cassol VJ, Badler NI, Musse SR, Jung CR (2017) Detection of global and local motion changes in human crowds. IEEE Trans Circ Syst Video Technol 27(3):603–612

Dee HM, Caplier A (2010) Crowd behaviour analysis using histograms of motion direction. In: IEEE international conference on image processing (ICIP), pp 1545–1548

Dihl LL, Jung CR, Bins JC (2011) Robust adaptive patch-based object tracking using weighted vector median filters. In: Conference on graphics, patterns and images (SIBGRAPI), pp 149–156

Dollar P, Wojek C, Schiele B, Perona P (2012) Pedestrian detection: an evaluation of the state of the art. IEEE Trans Pattern Anal Mach Intell 34(4):743–761

Edney JJ, Grundmann MJ (1979) Friendship, group size and boundary size: small group spaces. Small Group Res 124–135

Enzweiler M, Gavrila DM (2009) Monocular pedestrian detection: survey and experiments. IEEE Trans Pattern Anal Mach Intell 31(12):2179–2195

Fagot-Bouquet L, Audigier R, Dhome Y, Lerasle F (2016) Improving multi-frame data association with sparse representations for robust near-online multi-object tracking. In: European conference on computer vision, Springer, pp 774–790

Fawcett T (2006) An introduction to roc analysis. Pattern Recogn Lett 27(8):861–874

Felzenszwalb P, McAllester D, Ramanan D (2008) A discriminatively trained, multiscale, deformable part model. In: IEEE conference on computer vision and pattern recognition, 2008. CVPR 2008. IEEE, pp 1–8

Feng L, Bhanu B (2015) Understanding dynamic social grouping behaviors of pedestrians. IEEE J Sel Top Sign Proces 9:317–329

Fenwick M, BornØ T, Favre T, Tusell J (2011) UEFA guide to quality stadiums. Union of European Football Associations (UEFA), Nyon, Switzerland

Ferryman J, Ellis A (2010) Pets2010: Dataset and challenge. In: Advanced video and signal based surveillance

Ferryman J, Shahrokni A (2009) Pets2009: Dataset and challenge. In: Twelfth IEEE international workshop on performance evaluation of tracking and surveillance (PETS-Winter), 2009. IEEE, pp 1–6

Fleuret F, Berclaz J, Lengagne R, Fua P (2008) Multi-camera people tracking with a probabilistic occupancy map. IEEE Trans Pattern Anal Mach Intell 30(2):267–282

Fradi H, Luvison B, Pham QC (2017) Crowd behavior analysis using local mid-level visual descriptors. IEEE Trans Circuits Syst Video Technol 27(3):589–602

Freud S (1922) Group psychology and the analysis of the ego. Boni and Liveright, New York

Fruin J (1971a) Pedestrian and planning design. Metropolitan association of urban designers and environmental planners., Elevator World Inc. Educational Services Division. PO Box 6507, 354 Morgan Avenue, Mobile, Alabama 36606

Fruin J (1971b) Pedestrian planning and design. Metropolitan Association of Urban Designers and Environmental Planners

Fruin JJ (1971c) Designing for pedestrians: a level of service concept. Highway Res Rec 355:1–15

Führ G, Jung CR (2014) Combining patch matching and detection for robust pedestrian tracking in monocular calibrated cameras. Pattern Recogn Lett 39:11–20

Führ G, Jung CR (2012) Robust patch-based pedestrian tracking using monocular calibrated cameras. In: Conference on graphics, patterns and images (SIBGRAPI), pp 166–173

Fu L, Song W, Lv W, Lo S (2014) Simulation of exit selection behavior using least effort algorithm. Transportation Research Procedia 2(0):533–540. https://doi.org/10.1016/j.trpro.2014.09.093. http://www.sciencedirect.com/science/article/pii/S235214651400129X, the Conference on Pedestrian and Evacuation Dynamics 2014 (PED 2014), 22–24 October 2014, Delft, The Netherlands

Galea ER (1998) A general approach to validating evacuation models with an application to EXODUS. J Fire Sci 16(6):414–436

Ge W, Collins RT, Ruback RB (2012) Vision-based analysis of small groups in pedestrian crowds. Pattern Anal Mach Intell 34(5):1003–1016

Granger CW (1969) Investigating causal relations by econometric models and cross-spectral methods. Econometrica: J Econometric Soc 424–438

Grant JM, Flynn PJ (2017) Crowd scene understanding from video: a survey. ACM Trans Multimedia Comput Commun Appl (TOMM) 13(2):19

Guy SJ, van den Berg J, Liu W, Lau R, Lin MC, Manocha D (2012) A statistical similarity measure for aggregate crowd dynamics. ACM Trans Graph 31(6):190:1–190:11. https://doi.org/10.1145/2366145.2366209. http://doi.acm.org/10.1145/2366145.2366209

Gwynne S, Galea ER, Owen M, Lawrence PJ, Filippidis L (1999) A review of the methodologies used in the computer simulation of evacuation from the built environment. Build Environ 34:741–749

Hall ET (1959) The silent language. Doubleday Company, Garden City, NY

Hall ET (1966) The hidden dimension, 1st edn. Doubleday, Garden City, NY

Haque M, Murshed MM (2010) Panic-driven event detection from surveillance video stream without track and motion features. In: IEEE international conference on multimedia and expo, pp 173–178

Haritaoglu I, Harwood D, Davis L (1998) W4 s: a real-time system for detecting and tracking people in 2 1/2d. Eur Conf Comput Vision 1406:877–892

Haron F, Alginahi YM, Kabir MN, Mohamed AI (2012) Software evaluation for crowd evacuation software evaluation for crowd evacuation–case study: Al case study: Al case study: Al-masjid an masjid an-nabawi. Int J Comput Sci Issues (IJCSI)

Hart PE, Nilsson NJ, Raphael B (1972) A formal basis for the heuristic determination of minimum cost paths. SIGART Bull 37:28–29. http://doi.acm.org/10.1145/1056777.1056779

Helbing D, Farkas I, Vicsek T (2000) Simulating dynamical features of escape panic. Nature 407:487–490. http://arxiv.org/abs/cond-mat/0009448,cond-mat/0009448

Helbing D, Molnár P (1995) Social force model for pedestrian dynamics. Phys Rev E 51:4282–4286. https://doi.org/10.1103/PhysRevE.51.4282. https://link.aps.org/doi/10.1103/PhysRevE.51.4282

Helbing D, Molnar P (1998) Self-organization phenomena in pedestrian crowds. ArXiv Condensed Matter e-prints arXiv:cond-mat/9806152

Huang P, Kang J, Kider JT, Sunshine-Hill B, McCaffrey JB, Rios DV, Badler NI (2010) Real-time evacuation simulation in mine interior model of smoke and action. In: The 23rd annual conference on computer animation and social agents

Hurley MJ, Gottuk DT, Hall JR Jr, Harada K, Kuligowski ED, Puchovsky M, Torero JL, Watts JM Jr, Wieczorek CJ (2015) SFPE handbook of fire protection engineering, 5th edn. National Fire Protection Association, London, UK

Idrees H, Saleemi I, Seibert C, Shah M (2013) Multi-source multi-scale counting in extremely dense crowd images. In: Proceedings of the IEEE conference on computer vision and pattern recognition, pp 2547–2554

International Code Council (2012) Means of egress. In: International building code, United States, pp 217–254

International Maritime Organization (2007) Guidelines for evacuation analysis for new and existing passenger ships. Marine Safety Committee, London

Jacques Junior J, Musse S, Jung C (2010) Crowd analysis using computer vision techniques. IEEE Sign Proces Mag 27(5):66–77

Jacques JCS Jr, Braun A, Soldera J, Musse SR, Jung CR (2007) Understanding people motion in video sequences using voronoi diagrams. Pattern Anal Appl 10(4):321–332

Jiang L, Li J, Shen C, Yang S, Han Z (2014) Obstacle optimization for panic flow–reducing the tangential momentum increases the escape speed. PLoS ONE 9(12):1–15. https://doi.org/10.1371/journal.pone.0115463. http://dx.doi.org/10.1371

Ji L, Qian Y, Zeng J, Wang M, Xu D, Yan Y, Feng S (2013) Simulation of evacuation characteristics using a 2-dimensional cellular automata model for pedestrian dynamics. J Appl Math

Jones MJ, Snow D (2008) Pedestrian detection using boosted features over many frames. In: Proceedings of the international conference on pattern recognition, pp 1–4

Kaltsa V, Briassouli A, Kompatsiaris I, Hadjileontiadis L, Strintzis M (2015) Swarm intelligence for detecting interesting events in crowded environments. IEEE Trans Image Process 24(7):2153–2166. https://doi.org/10.1109/TIP.2015.2409559

Kanyuk P (2017) Virtual crowds in film and narrative media. In: Pelechano N, Albeck JM, Kapadia M, Badler NI (eds) Simulating heterogeneous crowds with interactive behaviors, CRC Press, USA, Chap. 10, pp 217–234

Kendon A (1977) Studies in the behavior of social interaction. Peter De Ridder Press, Lisse

Kong D, Gray D, Tao H (2006) A viewpoint invariant approach for crowd counting. Proceedings of the international conference on pattern recognition 3:1187–1190. http://doi.ieeecomputersociety.org/10.1109/ICPR.2006.197

Korhonen T, Hostikka S, Heliövaara S, Ehtamo H (2009) Fds+evac: An agent based fire evacuation model. Pedestrian and Evacuation Dynamics, Springer, Berlin Heidelberg, Chap. 8:109–120. https://doi.org/10.1007/978-3-642-04504-2_8

Kratz L, Nishino K (2012) Going with the flow: pedestrian efficiency in crowded scenes. Comput Vision-ECCV 2012:558–572

Kuligowski E, Gwynne S (2005) What a user should know when selecting an evacuation model. Fire Protection Engeneering, pp 600–611. http://magazine.sfpe.org/occupants-and-egress/what-user-should-know-when-selecting-evacuation-model

Leal-Taixé L, Milan A, Reid I, Roth S, Schindler K (2015) Motchallenge 2015: Towards a benchmark for multi-target tracking. arXiv preprint arXiv:150401942

LeBon G (1895) Psychologie des Foules. Alcan, Paris

LeCun Y, Bengio Y, Hinton G (2015) Deep learning. Nature 521(7553):436–444

Lee D, Suk HI, Park SK, Lee SW (2015) Motion influence map for unusual human activity detection and localization in crowded scenes. IEEE Trans Circuits Syst Video Technol 25(10):1612–1623

Leibe E Band Seemann, Schiele B (2005) Pedestrian detection in crowded scenes. In: Proceedings of IEEE conference on computer vision and pattern recognition, Washington, DC, USA, pp 878–885

Lepetit V, Fua P (2005) Monocular model-based 3d tracking of rigid objects: A survey. Foundations and trends in computer graphics and vision 1(CVLAB-ARTICLE-2005-002):1–89

Lerner A, Chrysanthou Y, Lischinski D (2007) Crowds by example. Computer Graphics Forum, Wiley Online Library 26:655–664

Li W, Mahadevan V, Vasconcelos N (2014) Anomaly detection and localization in crowded scenes. IEEE Trans Pattern Anal Mach Intell 36(1):18–32

Li T, Chang H, Wang M, Ni B, Hong R, Yan S (2015) Crowded scene analysis: A survey. IEEE Trans Circuits Syst Video Technol 25(3):367–386

Lin SF, Chen JY, Chao HX (2001) Estimation of number of people in crowded scenes using perspective transformation. IEEE Trans Syst Man Cybern-Part A 31(6):645–654

Liu W, Chong X, Huang P, Badler NI (2014) Learning motion patterns in unstructured scene based on latent structural information. J Visual Lang Comput 25(1):43–53

Ma R, Li L, Huang W, Tian Q (2004) On pixel count based crowd density estimation for visual surveillance. Proceedings of the IEEE conference on cybernetics and intelligent systems 1:170–173

Marana A, da Costa L, Lotufo R, Velastin S (1998) On the efficacy of texture analysis for crowd monitoring. In: SIBGRAPI '98: proceedings of the international symposium on computer graphics, image processing, and vision, Washington, DC, USA, p 354

Mc Dougall W (2009) The group mind (1920). Lightning Source, La Vergne, US

McPhail C (1991) The myth of the madding crowd. Walter de Gruyter, New York, USA

McPhail C, Wohlstein RT (1982) Using film to analyze pedestrian behavior. Sociol Methods Res 10(3):347–375

Mehran R, Oyama A, Shah M (2009) Abnormal crowd behavior detection using social force model. In: IEEE conference on computer vision and pattern recognition, pp 935–942

Milan A, Leal-Taixé L, Reid I, Roth S, Schindler K (2016) Mot16: a benchmark for multi-object tracking. arXiv preprint arXiv:160300831

Milgram S, Toch H, Drury J (1969) Collective behavior: crowds and social movements

Moore SC, Flajslik M, Rosin PL, Marshall D (2008) A particle model of crowd behavior: Exploring the relationship between alcohol, crowd dynamics and violence. Aggression and Violent Behavior 13(6):413–422. https://doi.org/10.1016/j.avb.2008.06.004. http://www.sciencedirect.com/science/article/pii/S1359178908000451

Murphy SO, Brown KN, Sreenan C (2013) The evacsim pedestrian evacuation agent model: development and validation. In: Proceedings of the 2013 summer computer simulation conference, society for modeling and simulation international, Vista, CA, SCSC '13, pp 38:1–38:8. URL:http://dl.acm.org/citation.cfm?id=2557696.2557737

Mu H, Wang J, Mao Z, Sun J, Lo S, Wang Q (2013) Pre-evacuation human reactions in fires: an attribution analysis considering psychological process. Procedia Eng 52:290–296. https://doi.org/10.1016/j.proeng.2013.02.142. http://www.sciencedirect.com/science/article/pii/S1877705813002610, 2012 International Conference on Performance-based Fire and Fire Protection Engineering

NFPA 101 Life Safety Code, (2015) National Fire Protection Association. Quincy, MA

Osorio LC (2003) Psicologia Grupal: Uma nova disciplina para o advento de uma era. Artmed, Porto Alegre

Ottonello C, Peri M, Regazzoni C, Tesei A (1992) Integration of multisensor data for overcrowding estimation. IEEE international conference on systems, man and cybernetics 1:791–796. https://doi.org/10.1109/ICSMC.1992.271529

Patil S, Van Den Berg J, Curtis S, Lin M, Manocha D (2011) Directing crowd simulations using navigation fields. IEEE Trans Visual Comput Graphics 17(2):244–254. https://doi.org/10.1109/TVCG.2010.33

Pelechano N, O'Brien K, Silverman B, Badler N (2005) Crowd simulation incorporating agent psychological models, roles and communication. Tech. rep, DTIC Document

Pelechano N, Allbeck JM, Kapadia M, Badler NI (2016) Simulating heterogeneous crowds with interactive behaviors. CRC Press

Pelechano N, Allbeck J, Badler N (2008) Virtual crowds: methods, simulation, and control (synthesis lectures on computer graphics and animation). Morgan and Claypool Publishers

Pelechano N, Badler NI (2006) Modeling crowd and trained leader behavior during building evacuation. IEEE Comput Graphics Appl 26(6):80–86. https://doi.org/10.1109/MCG.2006.133

Pelechano N, Malkawi A (2008) Evacuation simulation models: challenges in modeling high rise building evacuation with cellular automata approaches. Autom Constr 17(4):377–385. https://doi.org/10.1016/j.autcon.2007.06.005. http://www.sciencedirect.com/science/article/pii/S0926580507000908

Pillac V, Van Hentenryck P, Even C (2014) A path-generation matheuristic for large scale evacuation planning. In: Blesa M, Blum C, Voss S (eds) Hybrid metaheuristics, lecture notes in computer science, vol 8457, Springer International Publishing, pp 71–84. https://doi.org/10.1007/978-3-319-07644-7_6

Pirsiavash H, Ramanan D, Fowlkes CC (2011) Globally-optimal greedy algorithms for tracking a variable number of objects. In: IEEE conference on computer vision and pattern recognition, pp 1201–1208

Police Executive Research Forum (2011) Managing major events: best practices from the field. Critical issues in policing series, Police Executive Research Forum

Polícia Militar do Estado de São Paulo (2004) Dimensionamento de Lotação e Saídas de Emergência em Centros Esportivos e de Exibição. Secretaria de Estado dos Negócios e da Segurança Publica, São Paulo, Brazil

Rabaud V, Belongie S (2006) Counting crowded moving objects. In: Proceedings of the IEEE conference on computer vision and pattern recognition, pp 705–711. https://doi.org/10.1109/CVPR.2006.92

Rahmalan H, Nixon M, Carter J (2006) On crowd density estimation for surveillance. In: Proceedings of the institution of engineering and technology conference on crime and security, pp 540–545

Regazzoni CS, Tesei A, Murino V (1993) A real-time vision system for crowding monitoring. Proceedings of the international conference on industrial electronics, control, and instrumentation 3:1860–1864

Ren A, Chen C, Shi J, Zou L (2006) Application of virtual reality technology to evacuation simulation in fire disaster. In: Arabnia HR (ed) CGVR, CSREA Press, pp 15–21. http://dblp.uni-trier.de/db/conf/cgvr/cgvr2006.html#RenCSZ06

Reynolds CW (1987) Flocks, herds and schools: a distributed behavioral model. In: SIGGRAPH '87: proceedings of the 14th annual conference on computer graphics and interactive techniques, ACM, New York, NY, USA, pp 25–34. http://doi.acm.org/10.1145/37401.37406

Rittsche J, Tu PH, Krahnstoeve N (2005) Simultaneous estimation of segmentation and shape. Proceedings of computer vision and pattern recognition, Washington, DC, USA 2:486–493

Rodriguez M, Ali S, Kanade T (2009) Tracking in unstructured crowded scenes. In: Proceedings of IEEE international conference on computer vision, Kyoto, Japan

Rodriguez M, Sivic J, Laptev I, Audibert JY (2011) Data-driven crowd analysis in videos. In: 2011 IEEE international conference on computer vision (ICCV), IEEE, pp 1235–1242

Rodriguez S, Zhang Y, Gans N, Amato NM (2013) Optimizing aspects of pedestrian traffic in building designs. In: 2013 IEEE/RSJ international conference on intelligent robots and systems (IROS), pp 1327–1334. https://doi.org/10.1109/IROS.2013.6696521

Ronchi E, Kinsey M (2011) Evacuation models of the future: insights from an online survey on user's experiences and needs. In: Capote J, Alvear D (eds) Proceedings of the advanced research workshop: evacuation and human behaviour in emergency situations, Universidad de Cantabria, pp 145–155

Ryan D, Denman S, Sridharan S, Fookes C (2015) An evaluation of crowd counting methods, features and regression models. Comput Vis Image Underst 130:1–17

Schatz K, Schlittenlacher J, Ullrich D, Ruppel U, Ellermeier W (2014) Investigating human factors in fire evacuation: a serious-gaming approach. In: Weidmann U, Kirsch U, Schreckenberg M (eds) Pedestrian and evacuation dynamics 2012, Springer International Publishing, pp 1113–1121. https://doi.org/10.1007/978-3-319-02447-9_91

Shao J, Change Loy C, Wang X (2014) Scene-independent group profiling in crowd. In: Proceedings of the IEEE conference on computer vision and pattern recognition, pp 2219–2226

Shao J, Kang K, Change Loy C, Wang X (2015) Deeply learned attributes for crowded scene understanding. In: Proceedings of the IEEE conference on computer vision and pattern recognition, pp 4657–4666

Shao J, Loy CC, Wang X (2016) Learning scene-independent group descriptors for crowd understanding. In: IEEE transactions on circuits and systems for video technology

Shi J, Tomasi C (1994) Good features to track. In: IEEE conference on computer vision and pattern recognition, pp 593–600

Sighele S (1954) A multidão Criminosa - Ensaio de Psicologia Coletiva. Tradução Adolfo Lima

Silverman BG, Johns M, Cornwell J, O'Brien K (2006) Human behavior models for agents in simulators and games: Part I: enabling science with PMFserv. Presence Teleoper Virtual Environ 15(2):139–162. https://doi.org/10.1162/pres.2006.15.2.139

Singh S, Kapadia M, Hewlett B, Reinman G, Faloutsos P (2011) A modular framework for adaptive agent-based steering. In: Symposium on interactive 3D graphics and games, ACM, New York,

NY, USA, I3D '11, pp 141–150. https://doi.org/10.1145/1944745.1944769. http://doi.acm.org/
    10.1145/1944745.1944769

Smeulders AW, Chu DM, Cucchiara R, Calderara S, Dehghan A, Shah M (2014) Visual tracking:
    an experimental survey. IEEE Trans Pattern Anal Mach Intell 36(7):1442–1468

Solera F, Calderara S, Cucchiara R (2016) Socially constrained structural learning for groups detec-
    tion in crowd. IEEE Trans Pattern Anal Mach Intell 38(5):995–1008

Solmaz B, Moore BE, Shah M (2012) Identifying behaviors in crowd scenes using stability analysis
    for dynamical systems. IEEE Trans Pattern Anal Mach Intell 34(10):2064–2070

Stewart R, Andriluka M, Ng AY (2016) End-to-end people detection in crowded scenes. In: Pro-
    ceedings of the IEEE conference on computer vision and pattern recognition, pp 2325–2333

Still GK (2000) Crowd dynamics. PhD thesis, University of Warwick, Coventry, UK

Su H, Yang H, Zheng S, Fan Y, Wei S (2013) The large-scale crowd behavior perception based on
    spatio-temporal viscous fluid field. IEEE Trans Inf Forensics Secur 8(10):1575–1589

Thalmann D, Musse SR (2013) Crowd Simulation, 2nd edn. Springer, London

University of Minnesota: Unusual Crowd Activity Dataset (2006). http://www.mha.cs.umn.edu/
    movies/crowd-activity-all.avi

van den Berg J, Guy SJ, Lin MC, Manocha D (2009) Reciprocal n-body collision avoidance. In:
    Pradalier C, Siegwart R, Hirzinger G (eds) ISRR, Springer, Springer Tracts in Advanced Robotics,
    vol 70, pp 3–19. http://dblp.uni-trier.de/db/conf/isrr/isrr2009.html#BergGLM09

Van den Berg J, Lin M, Manocha D (2008) Reciprocal velocity obstacles for real-time multi-agent
    navigation. In: IEEE international conference on robotics and automation, 2008, ICRA 2008.
    IEEE, pp 1928–1935

Wang W, Lin W, Chen Y, Wu J, Wang J, Sheng B (2014) Finding coherent motions and seman-
    tic regions in crowd scenes: a diffusion and clustering approach. In: European conference on
    computer vision, Springer, pp 756–771

Wang H, Ondřej J, O'Sullivan C (2016) Path patterns: Analyzing and comparing real and simulated
    crowds. In: Proceedings of the 20th ACM SIGGRAPH symposium on interactive 3D graphics
    and games, ACM, New York, NY, USA, I3D '16, pp 49–57. https://doi.org/10.1145/2856400.
    2856410. http://doi.acm.org/10.1145/2856400.2856410

World Health Organization (2007) Drinking and driving: a road safety manual for decision-makers
    and practitioners. Global Road Safety Partnership, Geneva. http://www.who.int/roadsafety/
    projects/manuals/alcohol/drinking_driving.pdf

Wu S, Wong HS, Yu Z (2014) A bayesian model for crowd escape behavior detection. IEEE Trans
    Circuits Syst Video Technol 24(1):85–98

Wu X, Liang G, Lee KK, Xu Y (2006) Crowd density estimation using texture analysis and learning.
    In: Proceedings of the IEEE international conference on robotics and biomimetics, pp 214–219

Wu S, Moore BE, Shah M (2010) Chaotic invariants of lagrangian particle trajectories for anomaly
    detection in crowded scenes. In: IEEE conference on computer vision and pattern recognition,
    pp 2054–2060

Wu B, Nevatia R (2006) Tracking of multiple, partially occluded humans based on static body part
    detection. In: 2006 IEEE computer society conference on computer vision and pattern recognition,
    IEEE, vol 1, pp 951–958

Xi M, Smith SP (2015) Exploring the reuse of fire evacuation behaviour in virtual environments.
    In: Pisan NKY, Blackmore K (eds) 11th Australasian conference on interactive entertainment
    (IE 2015), ACS, Sydney, Australia, CRPIT, vol 167, pp 35–44. http://crpit.com/confpapers/
    CRPITV167Xi.pdf

Yang DB, Héctor H González-Ba n, Guibas LJ (2003) Counting people in crowds with a real-
    time network of simple image sensors. In: Proceedings of the IEEE international conference on
    computer vision, Washington, DC, USA, p 122

Yi S, Wang X, Lu C, Jia J, Li H (2016) L0 regularized stationary-time estimation for crowd analysis.
    IEEE Trans Pattern Anal Mach Intell 39(5):981–2017

Yilmaz A, Javed O, Shah M (2006) Object tracking: a survey. ACM CSUR 38(4):1–45

Yogameena B, Nagananthini C (2017) Computer vision based crowd disaster avoidance system: a survey. Int J Disaster Risk Reduction

Zhan B, Monekosso DN, Remagnino P, Velastin SA, Xu LQ (2008) Crowd analysis: a survey. Mach Vis Appl 19(5–6):345–357

Zhang C, Li H, Wang X, Yang X (2015) Cross-scene crowd counting via deep convolutional neural networks. In: Proceedings of the IEEE conference on computer vision and pattern recognition, pp 833–841

Zhang C, Kang K, Li H, Wang X, Xie R, Yang X (2016a) Data-driven crowd understanding: a baseline for a large-scale crowd dataset. IEEE Trans Multimedia 18(6):1048–1061

Zhang Y, Zhou D, Chen S, Gao S, Ma Y (2016b) Single-image crowd counting via multi-column convolutional neural network. In: Proceedings of the IEEE conference on computer vision and pattern recognition, pp 589–597

Zhao T, Nevatia R (2003) Bayesian human segmentation in crowded situations. Proceedings of the IEEE conference on computer vision and pattern recognition 2:459–466

Zhao X, Gong D, Medioni G (2012) Tracking using motion patterns for very crowded scenes. Computer Vision-ECCV 2012:315–328

Zhou B, Tang X, Wang X (2013) Measuring crowd collectiveness. In: Proceedings of the IEEE conference on computer vision and pattern recognition, pp 3049–3056

Zhou B, Tang X, Wang X (2015) Learning collective crowd behaviors with dynamic pedestrian-agents. Int J Comput Vision 111(1):50–68

Zhu N, Wang J, Shi J (2008) Application of pedestrian simulation in olympic games. J Transp Syst Eng Inf Tech 8(6):85–90. https://doi.org/10.1016/S1570-6672(09)60007-6. http://www.sciencedirect.com/science/article/B8H0W-4VDRVV0-7/2/3ff342f75f2deb5c1acdb0484b75e002

Zhou B, Wang X, Tang X (2012) Understanding collective crowd behaviors: learning a mixture model of dynamic pedestrian-agents. In: IEEE conference on computer vision and pattern recognition, IEEE, pp 2871–2878

Printed in the United States
By Bookmasters